MEMOIRS
of the
BASTILLE

The Annotated Version

Simon-Nicolas-Henri Linguet

With notes and an introduction by Jim Chevallier

Notes, introduction and graphics copyright © 2005 by Jim Chevallier

All rights reserved, including the right of reproduction in any form.

Although the editor and publisher have made every effort to ensure the accuracy and completeness of this transcription and any additional information contained in this book, we assume no responsibility for errors, inaccuracies, omissions, or any inconsistency herein.

To contact the editor, e-mail: *jimchev@chezjim.com*

Published by:
Chez Jim Books

Other books written, edited or translated by Jim Chevallier:

- The Old Regime Police Blotter I: Bloodshed, Sex and Violence in Pre-Revolutionary France
- The Old Regime Police Blotter II: Sodomites, Tribads and "Crimes Against Nature"
- Après Moi Le Dessert I: A French eighteenth century model meal
- Après Moi Le Dessert II: A French eighteenth century vegetarian meal
- How To Cook A Peacock: Le Viandier - Medieval Recipes by Taillevent
- Monologues for Teens and Twenties
- Thirty Monologues for Teens
- Suicide Monologues for Actors and Others

Jim Chevallier is also a contributor to the *Dictionnaire Universel du Pain* (Laffont, 2010). His photographs of the winemakers of Chablis can be seen in *The Wines of Chablis and the Yonne* by Rosemary George.

ISBN: *978-1-4563-2625-8*

ABOUT THE TEXT AND COVER
The original text of this anonymous translation was published in Dublin in 1783. The cover illustration is from an 1878 print of the Bastille as it was in 1420. For the quote on the back cover, see "About This Work".

CONTENTS

ABOUT THIS WORK I

ABOUT LINGUET V

NOTES FOR THE MODERN READER X
    A WORD ON NOTES X

ADVERTISEMENT FOR THE TRANSLATOR I

MEMOIRS OF THE BASTILLE 1
    PART I 1
        SECTION I 7
        SECTION II 16
        NOTES 37
    PART II 53
        SECTION III 53
            Secrecy of imprisonment 57
            Ignorance of the outside world 61
            Prisoners incommunicado 63
            Arrival at the Bastille 65
            Cells 66
            Inadequate heat 67
            Furniture and decoration 69
            Isolation of prisoners 72
            Sharp objects: suicide and shaving 76
            Turn-keys 79
            Lack of diversion 80
            Rates and revenues 82
            Fear of poisoning 84
            Tours for visitors 87
            Limits on exercise 88
            Chained figures on the clock 89
            The "closet" 90
            More on secret custody 92
            Illness 94
            Mass, confession and death 99
            Hope mocked 101
            Denied a will 103
            Types of prisoners 105
            Special treatment 107
            In the name of the King… 110
    NOTES 113

APPENDICES 145
    APPENDIX A. INTAKE AND EXIT FORMS 145
    APPENDIX B. THE LAYOUT OF THE BASTILLE 146

APPENDIX C. FOOD IN THE BASTILLE 151
APPENDIX D. PELLISERI'S LETTER TO MAJOR LOSMES 157

BIBLIOGRAPHY **161**

THE BASTILLE 161
    BOOK-LENGTH MEMOIRS ON THE BASTILLE *161*
    ACCOUNTS OF THE BASTILLE INCLUDED IN MEMOIRS *162*
    OTHER SOURCES ON THE BASTILLE *163*
LINGUET 164
    BIOGRAPHIES AND STUDIES *164*
SOURCES ON 17TH AND 18TH CENTURY FRANCE 165
LEGAL AND SOCIAL TEXTS 165
OTHER COUNTRIES 165
REFERENCE 166
WEB SITES 166

ILLUSTRATIONS

Portrait of Linguet by Saint-Aubin, 1773 .... *iv*
Frontispiece of the original English translation .... *xii*
A page from the original translation .... *iii*
View of the Bastille from the west *148*
View of the Bastille from the southeast *148*

About This Work

Like the folksinger Woody Guthrie, Simon-Nicolas-Henri Linguet was born on Bastille Day, the day (July 14) when the French celebrate the storming of the Bastille. Like Guthrie, too, the lawyer-turned-journalist Linguet eloquently protested injustice. Unlike Guthrie, Linguet had been in the Bastille, and, with this book, may have helped bring it down.

This was not the first book to offer a peek inside that notorious prison. Though few who left the place wrote about it, over two centuries other accounts had been published. At the start of the century, Renneville in particular had, like Linguet, immediately fled to England and written a book about his experience. Others had described the prison in their memoirs.

But in 1783, when this work first appeared, France was in ferment and closer than most knew to a revolution. The French king had just helped the American colonists win their independence. Absolute power was going out of style.

Nor had Linguet been just any prisoner, or just any writer. He was personally famous (or infamous), but more importantly he was the editor of one of the most eagerly read periodicals of the times. He first published this work there, which in itself assured that it would be widely read.

What's more, his account was up to date. The Bastille Linguet describes here is essentially the same that would be destroyed six years later. Its governor – that is, its warden – was the same man who would defy the populace and be massacred for his pains.

In the discussions that followed this book's publication, not everybody accepted it uncritically. Linguet collected enemies, many of them writers, and he was not above exaggeration. But even the playwright La Harpe – whom Linguet had frequently attacked – in ending his critique acknowledged Linguet's central complaint: "It is nonetheless true that when he reproaches the government for having locked him up, instead of putting him on trial, he is unfortunately only too right." (He can't help adding, a little acidly, that "It is hard to be wrong [when opposing] Linguet.") (*Corrèspondance Littèraire*, IV 120.)

Fortunately, Linguet's most questionable statements *sound* dubious; as when he claims that he was poisoned, or, in a breath-taking note, itemizes some of the most awful punishments known to history and yet maintains that none are worse than the Bastille. With this, the footnotes in this new edition offer other perspectives on key points, giving the reader of this important historical document a rounded view of an institution whose fall, still today, symbolizes the birth of modern France.

Other ex-prisoners had written true memoirs, accounts of their own experience with the Bastille as a background. Linguet too begins with two chapters on his own history, leading up to his arrest. But in the third chapter – the one that takes us inside the Bastille – he writes like the lawyer he had been, methodically presenting a portrait of the prison meant to support one conclusion: the Bastille must be destroyed.

Barrière, co-editor of one French edition of this work, writes:

> Linguet dared tell all, and his *Memoir of the Bastille* contributed more than a little to the destruction of this fortress. He wrote it in 1782, only seven years before the first days of the revolution. Already signs warned of the storm; already a crowd of readers welcomed, with a greedy curiosity, reproaches, accusations and even outrages heaped upon authority. The true facts which Linguet's Memoir contains strengthened enlightened spirits in the desire to obtain from the powers-that-be themselves, concessions now necessary to the people's happiness: the declamations and the calumnies which this Memoir contains provoked the most audacious enterprises from men who were only too ready to destroy rather than reform. Linguet, by the fears he spread, the wishes he expressed, the works which his own inspired, accustomed people to the idea of overthrowing the Bastille. It was already conquered and destroyed in public opinion when the 14th of July arrived.
>
> *Mémoires de Linguet Sur la Bastille*, x-xi

Portrait of Linguet by Saint-Aubin, 1773

"In reality, Linguet was ugly, small and thin, nervous, with a jerky gait. One must see him in profile, with his vast forehead, eyebrows raised high, nose dry, lips thin and twisted, and, under clenched teeth, a devil of a chin which was the whole man."

Jean Cruppi, ***Un avocat journaliste du dix-huitième siècle, Linguet***

About Linguet

If you have heard of Simon-Nicolas-Henri Linguet at all, you probably know more about eighteenth-century France than is common. Even then, you might barely know his name, or only know him as someone who quarreled with a more illustrious figure; perhaps a playwright whose plays (unlike Linguet's) are still read, or a philosopher whose ideas (unlike Linguet's) are still studied, or an historian whose histories (unlike Linguet's)... You get the picture.

Linguet is, by most measures, unknown today. Already in the nineteenth century, a biographer wrote:

> Who would believe today that this man, wiped from history, filled Europe with his name, with the racket of his speech, his writings and his adventures? Who would believe that Voltaire dealt with him as an equal, that he was a god for Louis XVI, and the devil for his ministers, whom he never ceased to trouble; that he had held in check the Parliament, the Bar, the French Academy, the economic clan and all the leaders of philosophy; that, with immense success, he founded political journalism; that he was, in a word, one of the most talked about figures of the XVIII century?
>
> Jean Cruppi, *Un avocat journaliste du dix-huitième siècle, Linguet*, 2

When he wrote the present work, he was forty-six, and one of Europe's most famous journalists. He was at the height of his success, a success prompted by one of his greatest failures: as a lawyer.

As a lawyer, Linguet had lost more cases than he won, but was immensely popular with the public. His colleagues, however, hated him, and, in 1774, contrived to have him disbarred. If they'd expected to silence him, however, they'd made a terrible mistake. After several false starts as a journalist, he moved to London – out of reach of the royal censors – and started the *Annales politiques, civiles et littéraires du dix-huitième siècle*: "Political, civil and literary annals of the eighteenth century". It was a tremendous success – and often controversial. The abbé Morellet, who called him "a phony, a bad writer", saw in Linguet's thorny character the very key to his success: "[He] would never have been successful without the use he made of a powerful means to celebrity, *impudence*, ... whose full energy he understood better than anyone." (*Mèmoires*, I, 236). The remark is not entirely fair – Linguet was knowledgeable, eloquent and often (if harshly) witty – but not inaccurate either. As Darline Gay Levy puts it: "Linguet did not lack political enemies. In a sense, enemies were what he wanted. He almost courted antagonists on all sides the way more prudent and cunning men collected patrons and protectors." (*The Ideas and Careers of Simon-Henri Linguet*, 200).

Even Linguet's first fame as a lawyer had its roots in a conflict; one that, normally, would have been a footnote to his biography. In his late twenties, having failed as a playwright, a poet, an historian and even, incongruously, as a military man, he began to wander through Europe and ended up in Holland. Returning to France, he stopped in the northern town of Abbeville, where he drew the unwelcome attention of the mayor, Duval de Soicourt. But he also found a patron: Nicolas Douville de Maillefeu. Douville, a rival of Duval's, hired him as a tutor to his son and his upper-class young friends.

It took Linguet little time to again irritate the mayor, this time enough to be made distinctly unwelcome in the town. And so it was that, in 1764, he went to Paris to study law. He also wrote a work attacking the philosophers – Voltaire, et al – and, in dedicating it to Douville, said:

> Do not withdraw my name from the obscurity which it should never have left. What remains to me to live of a life poisoned early on by cruel sorrows, I consecrate to friendship,.....to retreat and above all to the study of man's true duties. (*Le fanatisme des philosophes*).

Within two years, and for decades after, that name would stand squarely in a very public glare.

While he was studying in Paris, a cross was mutilated in Abbeville. In the inquiry that followed, two of his former students were arrested. The inquiry was led by the now-former mayor, Duval de Soicourt, who soon ordered the arrest of Douville's son. How could Linguet not intervene?

Initially, he tried to free the first two young men, but was silenced. One – the Chevalier de la Barre – was tortured and executed. Linguet then wrote a memoir in defense of the others and, not yet a member of the bar, had it signed by a number of prominent lawyers. In the end, La Barre's friends were all freed. And Linguet had made a name for himself. It was 1766.

The remaining, not quite eight, years of Linguet's legal career were no less eventful (for which see Cruppi, Levy and others cited in the bibliography.) But his career as a journalist was monumental:

> Mounting a journalistic enterprise on an international scale, Linguet reestablished contact with his public and at the same time broadened the base of his support. He made the *Annales* into a quasi-independent force for molding opinion and policy in the power centers of Europe. Maneuvering among the great powers of Europe wielding the power of his public's opinion, Linguet institutionalized political influence for himself, and liberty as well... (Levy, 177).

In the process, he continued, usually unnecessarily, to make enemies, many of them powerful. For a detailed account of how he managed to offend the Duke de Duras (an Academician) and the rest of the French Academy, as well as the Secretary of State for foreign affairs (the Count de Vergennes), see Levy, 186-203. To resume the highlights of that account: after Linguet had offended the whole French Academy with his response to the induction of his enemy La Harpe, Duras had been one of two members of the Academy who had filed a complaint which resulted in Linguet's losing an earlier position as a journalist. When Duras was then involved in a civil suit, Linguet used the *Annales* to undermine Duras' position. Duras in turn had that issue of the *Annales* banned. Linguet's response was a vicious, if private, letter (dated

April 7, 1780), known only by second-hand reports. Duras, it seems, responded by having a *lettre-de-cachet* issued against Linguet, who was now in Brussels, having left England as hostilities grew with France.

Meanwhile, in trying to get the *Annales* officially sanctioned in France (they were ultimately only 'tolerated'), Linguet had written an aggressive letter to Vergennes (January 16, 1777). At first, Vergennes responded with good grace and even had the *Annales* sent to him (secretly). Linguet not only kept up the pressure but seems to have, in effect, tried to blackmail Vergennes and his fellow ministers (June 30, 1777). By the time Duras took action, Vergennes too had had enough. When Linguet wrote (as he tells us) for assurance that he could safely come to Paris, Vergennes twice (treacherously) reassured him. When Linguet did so, to meet with his literary agent, he was soon arrested and put in the Bastille: an experience detailed in these pages.

The success of this work was the high-point of Linguet's career. He was to have more adventures: he was made a noble by the (Austrian, not French) king; he offered his services as Louis XVI's lawyer; he became a mayor under the Revolution. But let us move past these and other tales to his life's tragic-comic end.

Despite the part played by this work in a key event of the Revolution, Linguet had written on so many subjects in so provocative a manner that he could be – and was – accused of holding anti-Revolutionary positions. As it happens, he was sick when he was arrested and was soon transferred to a hospital, where he might have stayed quietly out of harm's way. Instead, he once more wrote provocative letters, these to the Revolutionary tribunal, and demanded to be tried. Did he think his old eloquence as a lawyer would clear his name? If so, he had a sadly idealistic view of these summary courts. He was convicted and at once sent to the guillotine. Grumbling once again, it seems, about how unfairly he'd been treated.

Notes For The Modern Reader

The 'meat' of this work, for many readers, will be in the third chapter, which describes the experience of being in the Bastille. When Linguet first published his account, he could flatter himself that many readers were as interested in his personal travails – and in the then famous people he accuses – as they were in the Bastille itself. And so the first two chapters focus on the events and conflicts leading up to his imprisonment. Some today may want to skim or even skip these entirely.

Those with an interest in pre-Revolutionary France, however, should find them well worth reading. Not only do they mention figures who played parts in other major events, but they give a close-up view of the kind of quarrels that often intertwined the literary and political worlds of the time.

I have tried to preserve the feel of the original (and anonymous) English translation used here, keeping most of the English and/or archaic spellings, antiquated punctuation, etc. Since it is almost contemporaneous with the original French edition, this will give some sense of what English-speaking readers read at the time. For the third chapter only, I have added sub-headings to help the reader locate specific topics in regard to the Bastille.

A WORD ON NOTES

Linguet offers his own notes, in some cases as footnotes, indicated with the traditional *, †, ‡ marks, but more often as endnotes, indicated with numerals in parentheses: (1).

My own notes appear in two styles. General notes appear as endnotes, indicated with the standard numerals in superscript. Notes which specifically concern the Bastille or people in it appear as footnotes, indicated with the abbreviation BST in superscript, numbered (BST2) only where more than one note appears on the same page.

The original translator's rare notes are flagged with the notation *"Original translator's note"*. In regard to the translator's introduction, note that while Linguet was highly popular as a lawyer, he was frequently unsuccessful. Also, the "revolution" referred to was not the French Revolution, but a quarrel between Louis XV and the Parliament of Paris.

MEMOIRS
OF THE
BASTILLE.

Containing a FULL EXPOSITION of the
MYSTERIOUS POLICY
AND
DESPOTIC OPPRESSION
OF THE
FRENCH GOVERNMENT,
In the INTERIOR ADMINISTRATION of
THAT STATE-PRISON.
Interspersed with a Variety of
CURIOUS ANECDOTES.

*Non, mihi si voces centum sint, oraque centum
Omnia pœnarum percurrere nomina possim.* VIRG.

Translated from the FRENCH of
The Celebrated Mr. *LINGUET*,
Who was imprisoned there
From *September* 1780, to *May* 1782.

DUBLIN:
PRINTED BY J. A. HUSBAND,
FOR
Messrs. H. and W. WHITESTONE, WILSON,
MONCRIEFFE, WALKER, BURNET, WHITE,
EXSHAW, BYRNE, BURTON, CASH,
SLEATER, Junior, and PARKER.
M,DCC,LXXXIII.

Frontispiece of the original English translation

Advertisement

BY THE

TRANSLATOR

THIS work was wanting to the nomenclature of real State-Crimes; that is, of the sacrifices made by Despotism to the passions of its agents. The Author, Mr. LINGUET, was for ten years one of the most distinguished Counselors of the Parliament of *Paris*. He shone equally in oratory and composition. It has been remarked, that of a hundred and thirty Causes, all of them important, in which he had engaged during that period, he lost only nine. His enemies attribute this unparalleled success to the charms of his eloquence; his more candid judges, to the delicacy which directed him in the choice of his suits.

Whilst Mr. *Linguet* was thus displaying his useful and active talents at the Bar, he employed himself likewise in the cultivation of *Polite Literature,* and *Philosophy*. The boldness of his principles, the novelty of his views, and too great a freedom in his examination of the systems established and the facts prevailing in *France,* made him powerful enemies, even in the Ministry, in that Country, where as it is well known, there is at least as much cabal and party spirit as in our own; with this difference, that in *England* the objects are great, and the means public; whereas in *France* parties are formed and embittered for trifles, and mystery presides over intrigue.

In the revolution which some years ago interrupted all judicial order in *France,* Mr. *Linguet,* having suffered, on the part of the Parliament of *Paris,* and, ultimately, on that of Government itself, those shocking injuries of which the particulars may be seen in a work which he published three years ago, (*) sought an asylum in England. He there undertook a periodical work, intitled *Annales, Politiques, Civiles, & Littéraires du* 18ème *Siécle;* which met with a very favorable reception throughout *Europe.* This had been preceded by a printed Letter to the Count *de Vergennes,* one of the *French* Ministers, with whom he had most cause to be dissatisfied. This letter has been considered by the critics as a striking monument of energy, eloquence, and candour. It was of such a nature as to leave a deep and lasting impression on the mind; and it was sufficiently evident that it has not failed of this effect.

At the approach of the rupture between *England* and *France,* Mr. *Linguet,* having quitted the former, through a patriotic delicacy which has been been regretted, though not censured, by the *English;* and having persuaded himself, that on the *parole* of the-Count *de Vergennes* he might go to *France* to prosecute his interests there; he was arrested, on the 27th of *September* 1780, by virtue of a *Lettre-de-cachet,* and conducted to the *Bastille,* where he remained full twenty months.

This work contains the history of his imprisonment, that of the proceedings of those Ministers who have been accomplices in it, and a description of the regimen of that infernal institution equally celebrated and dreaded, but at the same time as little known as it is formidable.

---

* *Appel a la Posterité,* or the third volume of the Collection of Mr. *Linguet's* Works.

nefs and affection; that his end will perhaps be unknown; and that his miftaken wife and children may be offering up vows and making efforts for his deliverance, long after the sepulchre, in which he was buried alive will contain no remains of him but his bones!

Should we find such a picture in the voyages of Cooke, or Anson, what sort of impression would it make upon our minds? Might we not take the author for an impostor; or in felicitating ourselves on being natives of a country exempt from such a wretched servitude, should we not conceive a degree of contempt, mingled with horror, for a Government so barbarous, and a People so debased?

But, alas! it is the picture of no other than the BASTILLE, and that far from overcharged! How weakly does it represent those tortures and lengthened convulsions of the mind; those perpetual agonies that eternise the pains of death,

without:

A page from the original translation

Memoirs

of

THE BASTILLE

PART I.

London, Dec. 5, 1782.

I Am now in *England:* it is necessary to prove that my return hither has been a measure absolutely indispensable. – I am no longer at the *Bastille:* it is necessary to prove that I never deserved to be there. It is necessary to do more: to demonstrate that none have ever deserved it: the innocent, because they are innocent; the guilty, because they ought not to be convicted, judged, and punished, but according to the laws, and because at the *Bastille* none of the laws are observed, or rather they are all violated; because there are no tortures, unless perhaps in the infernal regions, which will bear to be set in competition with those of the *Bastille;* and because, if the institution itself may in certain cases admit of justification, it is impossible, in any case whatever, to justify the *regimen* of it. – It is necessary to show that this regimen, no less disgraceful than cruel, is equally repugnant to all the principles of justice, and humanity, to the manners of the Nation, to the mildness which characterizes the Royal House of *France,* and especially to the goodness, the equity of the Sovereign who at present fills the throne.

It is by this discussion that I am going to consecrate the renewal of my toils, my return to my painful career.

The two first articles seem to be merely personal, to

---

* I have been obliged to write many Notes, several of which are rather long. I have adopted the method of putting them at the end of the work, referring to them by corresponding figures. This method is less distracting to the Reader; and it will call to mind another work, where I have found it convenient to employ it.

concern none but myself. It will be seen however that they are inseparably connected with the third, and that they make an essential part of it. They form altogether a series of oppressions, a chain of iniquities and grievances, of which most assuredly very few instances are to be found since the History of Job.

Should I, in a word, be thought worthy to treat the last article, if I did not begin by clearing up the two others? Were I a mere miserable refugee, thirsting after vengeance, or a wretched criminal branded with the ignominy of a pardon, what weight would my claim, however urgent, carry with them?

But, after having seen the proofs of my innocence, the world will be more sensibly struck with the picture of those horrors from which that innocence has been insufficient to preserve me: their concern will still increase, when they reflect that there is not a *Frenchman,* nor even a Foreigner of those who visit the kingdom of *France,* who can assure himself that he shall not one day, in his own person experience those very horrors. The *Bastilles* of *France* have devoured, they are daily devouring, men of all ranks, and of all nations. At the avenues of these abysses (1) might well be engraven that memento which is sometimes seen inscribed to transitory readers on churchyard gates: *Hodie mihi, cras tibi!*

Who, in short, can promise himself that he shall escape that fate, from which the elevated rank of presumptive Heir to the Crown has not been sufficient to secure a *Louis* XII, nor their accumulated laurels a *Condé, (2)* or a *Luxemburg;* nor virtue, nor science, a *Sacy,* and so many others; nor the affected stateliness of the Long Robe, a *Pucelle;* nor the most important public services, a *La Bourdonnaie*[BST]; nor the right of nations so

---

[BST1] All these people, several highly placed, were imprisoned, most unjustly, most in the Bastille: Louis XII (1462-515) while still the Duke of Orleans took up arms against Charles VIII and was held in the tower of Bourges, after the battle of St. Aubin. (1488). He was held in an iron cage the first night and spent three years there. When he became king, he was urged to avenge himself on those responsible, but said, "It is not for the king of France to avenge the quarrels of the Duke of Orleans." *Biographie*

many *English, Germans, Italians, et.* whose names, engraven in fits of despondent weariness on all parts of those fatal walls, form a kind of geographic picture equally diversified and alarming, &c.? It is then, if I may use the expression, the character of an epidemic disease, formidable to all mankind, that I am going here to delineate. Notwithstanding the prodigious number of witnesses who have involuntarily visited these dungeons, the *minutiae* of their interior are very little known: the Memoirs of *La Porte*, of *Gourville*, of Mm. *de Staal*[BST2], give little or no information; the whole tending only

---

universelle XXV 181-185 —Louis II de Bourbon, Prince of Condé (1621-1686) had remained loyal to the Court during the first troubles of the Fronde, but was imprisoned in Vincennes for thirteen months (1650-1651), probably for opposing Mazarin. When he got out, he thought only of taking revenge on the Court. "I went into that prison the most innocent of men; I came out the most guilty." *Biographie universelle* IX, 11. —François-Henri de Montmorency, Count of Bouteville, Duke of Luxembourg (1628-1695), a Peer of the Realm, fell victim to accusations of witchcraft and poisoning and was sent to the Bastille (1679-1680). Though absolved, he was exiled for a year and never completely recovered his health. *Biographie universelle* XXV 317-519— Louis-Isaac Lemaistre de Sacy (or Saci) (1613-1684) was a Jansenist who was in the Bastille from 1666 to 1668. He is said to have begun his translation of the Bible there. He later said that young people were sent on voyages to form their minds, but that a little voyage of six months in the Bastille would do them far more good than a voyage of six years. Savine, 33; *Biographie universelle* XXXVII, 196-197. —The abbé Pucelle (1655-1745) was a counselor in Parliament and a fierce Jansenist who was exiled after conflicts with the powerful cardinal de Fleury (*Mémoires de Linguet* 4n).— Bernard François Mahé de la Bourdonnaie (1699-1755) was denounced, like General Lally, as a traitor for actions in India (in 1746). He spent three years in the Bastille before being cleared, and died soon after from the effects of his imprisonment. *Biographie universelle* XXVI, 61

[BST2] Three earlier memoirists who wrote about the Bastille (see Bibliography): Pierre de la Porte (1603-1680) was in the service of Anne of Austria, Louis XIII's wife, and served as an intermediary for her secret correspondence. Richelieu had him sent to the Bastille in 1637 in order to pressure him to betray the queen. He remained faithful however and, when her reconciliation with the king resulted in a pregnancy, he was released in 1638. *Biographie universelle* XXXIV 123. — L. Jean Hérault Sieur de Gourville, (1625-1703), a celebrated French financier, served, at different times, the Prince of Condé, Cardinal Mazarin and Louis XIV. He was briefly in the Bastille and wrote about it in his memoirs. Thomas, iv, 2345.—Marguerite Jeanne Delaunay, later (1735) Baronne de Staal

to prove a fact difficult to be conceived, that in their time this *Tartarus*, compared to what it is at present, was a kind of *Elysium*.

At that time the prisoners received visits, saw each other familiarly, and took their walks together; the Officers of the *Etat-Major* [BST] talked and eat with them; they were their comforters, no less than their guardians. *La Porte* speaks, in express terms, of the LIBERTIES OF THE BASTILLE; that is the name he gives to those alleviations which we have just mentioned, and which he and all his fellow-sufferers enjoyed.

And *La Porte* speaks of the reign of the *Cardinal Richelieu*: *La Porte* was, of all the men in the kingdom, the man the least to be treated with moderation. The relentless Minister was personally interested either in despotically wresting from him a valuable secret of which he was the confidant, or in vindictively tormenting him. The *Bastille* had therefore at that time no bitter portions of which he would not have drank, no tortures which he would not have undergone. Let his description be compared with mine. (3)

How has this increase of barbarism been effected? This I know not; but woeful experience has only too well assured me of its reality. Whilst the general manners seem in all respects to tend rather to softness than to rigor, whilst the reigning Prince discovers no views but such as are benevolent; whilst the sufferings even of criminal convicts have been abated, in the common prisons, by lenient regulations which his orders have produced; the only solicitude at the *Bastille* is to multiply tortures for the affliction of the innocent. The atrociousness of cruelty has been enhanced in this, more than it has been diminished in the other prisons.

(1684-1750); *Chambers*, 1740 (not to be confused with Mme de *Staël*, the pen name of Anne Louise Germaine Necker (1766-1817), a major literary figure of later years. *Benét's*, 975). Born poor, but educated well, she entered the service of the Duchess of Maine, who plotted against the regent. Delaunay (and *her* servant) were sent to the Bastille for two years as a result. *Chambers*, 1740.
[BST] Staff officers.

[5]

To reveal this inconceivable depravation is, under an equitable Prince, to render its reformation indispensable. Thus my last farewell to my country is an additional service which I shall render it; my last homage to the virtuous King who rules over it, will furnish him with a new occasion of doing that good, which constituting his delight, is the first object of his person.

But is there no interdict to prohibit the disclosure I am about to make? Can I without scruple treat the several subjects which I have engaged to discuss? Can I *in conscience* let the public into the secret of the terrible mysteries into which the 27th of September 1780 has initiated me?

The guardians of the *Bastille* have not indeed at their disposal the waters of *Lethe*[2], to cancel in the minds of their victims the remembrance of their cruelties; but they try to find a substitute for them. Despotism, which makes silence one of the torments of the *Bastille* during the period of confinement, endeavors, to make a religious duty of it at the termination of that period. Every *Jonas cast* forth from its jaws is compelled to SWEAR, *that he will never reveal, either directly or indirectly, a tittle of what he may have learnt or suffered there.*[BST]

It is a Magistrate in the habit apparently consecrated to justice, (4) it is men of the Military order, decorated with the external badge of an honourable service, (5) and of a life devoted to the defense of the citizens, who preside at this last act of an oppression of which they have been the instruments. Shewing the captive, half-revived, the door which alone can completely restore him to life, half-open, and ready instantly to close upon him again if he hesitates; they leave him no alternative, but those of silence, perjury, or death.

O ye well-informed of every Nation, rigid casuists who know what honour and delicacy prescribe, pronounce: Because my hands have been unjustly bound, must my pen be

---

[BST] Freed prisoners were literally made to swear. See the Exit (Liberty) form in Appendix A.

restrained too? Certainly not; with one united voice you decide that the infraction of that scandalous engagement is no perjury; that it is the exaction, not the violation of it, which constitutes the guilt.

You have absolved the celebrated Dellon[3] for having snapped the reins that had been fabricated by a religious Inquisition, which, having precisely the same principles as this political one, employs the same resources to bury the disgrace and the scandal of them. You are unanimous in renewing, and rendering for ever sacred, that axiom, so dear to society, that axiom, which, once forgotten, would give too unlimited a scope to miscreants armed with power, that the institution of an oath was intended to give stability to lawful conventions; to insure the observance of the laws; and not to defend, or assist in perpetuating, the abuses which infringe them.

SECTION I

My Return to England *a measure of necessity.*

AFTER what had passed in 1777 between the Count de Vergennes and me[4], (6) that Minister was, of all the Politicians in Europe, the one with whom I ought to have had the least concern. However, at the approach of the rupture between *France* and *England*, in March 1778, reckoning upon the reputation which he had acquired for personal delicacy and private probity, I thought I might run the risk of writing to him, to communicate my unwillingness to remain in a country which was going to become the enemy of my own: I requested to be informed whether, on changing my residence upon so patriotic a principle, I might not have new persecutions to apprehend from the *French* ministry. I concluded with these words: "I am perfectly sensible that the present situation of affairs will not permit me to indulge the hope of immediate reparation: but my heart would rest contented with that which the Public is making me, if, in transplanting myself, I could reckon on the enjoyment of repose; and I should reckon upon it. *if I had your word of honour as a pledge.*"

"You will pardon me, after my innocence has been well, perhaps too well, proved, that I think it necessary to take this precaution for my safety: but such is the misfortune of my position; and I dare believe that you will not be displeased with me on this account. If I distrust the Ministry, you see what confidence I place in the Minister."

The 20th of the same month, the Count *de Vergennes* answered me in these terms, "You communicated to me, Sir, *&c.* The Count *de Maurepas*[5], to whom I have imparted it, *entirely approves the resolution;* and he AUTHORIZES me to signify to you, that you may banish *all uneasiness on this head*; I think, Sir, that under this assurance you may take such steps as you shall judge most convenient. *I would not give it to you, if I did not absolutely consider it, myself, as very certain.*"

The 7th of April following, I asked of the Count *de Vergennes* a further explanation; I made a further sacrifice, more painful perhaps, more noble I can say with confidence, than even that of my residence. (7) The Count *de Vergennes*, the 23d, writes me for answer: "I have received, Sir, your letter; upon which I can only confirm to you what I have signified in my last, which announces to you, as well on the part of the Count *de Maurepas*, as on my own, an ENTIRE SAFETY FOR YOUR PERSON in the new habitation which you propose to yourself. I repeat to you very cordially the assurance of it, and that of *leaving it in your option to continue your literary labours;* being well convinced that neither the *King, Religion,* nor the *State,* will be attacked therein."

Upon this safeguard, solemn as we have just seen it, well authenticated, and totally unconditional, I quitted *England*. I settled at *Brussels*. I made several journeys to *France* in 1778 and 1779. I saw the Ministers. The *Annals* continued to have a circulation not less free than honourable; and I presume to say, that in no work which Literature has produced, have the *King, Religion,* and the *State* been more scrupulously respected.

The 27th of Sept. 1780, however, having been inveigled to *Paris* by a series of treacherous artifices, some of which I shall instance elsewhere, I found myself arrested in broad day-light, and this with studied and complicated circumstances of ignominy; (8) plunged into dungeons which in appearance are destined exclusively for the enemies of the *King,* or *Religion,* and of the *State;* and given up, in my person, in my honour, and in my fortune, to every indignity in which barbarous jailors, licentious calumniators, greedy prostitutes, and faithless agents, could indulge themselves.

At the expiration of twenty months, without any kind of mitigation, or explanation, my captivity apparently ended on the 19tb of May 1782; when in reality it only assumed a different form. The Lieutenant-general of the Police of *Paris,* coming with great parade to announce to me that I was no longer a *prisoner,* signified to me that I was *exiled:* he delivered me an order which banished me to a little town at the distance of forty leagues from *Paris,* with a prohibition to depart from it ON PAIN OF DISOBEDIENCE.

Though they did not deign to be more explicit on the motive of my *exile* than on that of my *imprisonment;* though I had the greatest reason to believe that this recent blow was leveled by the Ministry, not by the King, I submitted to it without demur. I asked only two favours very simple: the one, permission to stay at *Paris,* at least till I should have recovered strength sufficient to remove from it, and have drawn what was necessary for my subsistence out of hands more than suspicious, which by strange maneuvers were become possessed of almost all my property; the other, to go to spend some days at *Brussels,* in order to put an end to the confusion which for two years past had been mouldering away the rest of my fortune.

I ought the rather to have hoped for a compliance with these two requests, as the disorder I had to remedy proceeded directly from the *French* Ministry. They had caused to be *ministerially* demanded at *Brussels,* in the name of the *King of France,* by the *Chargé-d'affaires* of *France,* (9) seconded by an Exempt[6] of the Police of *Paris,* (10) and by a Deputy whom I shall elsewhere name (11) the remittance not only of *my papers,* but of *my money:* and what they did not carry away, they dissipated. They paid, at my expense, the excursions of the Under-minister, (12) of the Exempt in chief, of the Exempt *en second:* they paid a guard, whose service consisted in pillaging, under pretence of preserving: they paid the Officers of the country, eager to dispute with the foreign Officers the property of which they were despoiling me; and *French* injustice was lavish of my money towards the justice of *Brabant.*

Having, moreover, on the recovery of my existence, a new present to make to my country; having to give experimental proof of an invention extremely valuable[7]; to realize, for public utility, a project I had devised for rendering the light subservient to a purpose yet unknown, and that at a time when my eyes were strangers to it; the confidence with which I expected the modification, nay the revocation of my exile, was certainly not ill-founded.

Curiosity procured me a short respite on the first point; and it was not left ungratified. I made the experiment; it succeeded. (13) That very day, I received the injunction, *Depart for Rethel*, *and stir not, thence;* though in order to obtain permission to go to *Brussels,* I would have pledged myself, verbally, and in writing to return immediately; though for a month past I had incessantly renewed the promise, already offered from the bottom of my tomb, not, as some of the public prints have had the weakness or the malignity to give out, *to write only in subserviency to the views of The* French *Ministry,* but absolutely not to write any more, if that were required of me; to shut myself up in total silence, provided that, in lieu of this sacrifice, the common rights of a Citizen at least were restored to me; (14) provided that, for consenting to remain useless to society, since that was exacted of me, they would cease to treat me more rigorously than so many men who are a burden to it. I tempered, in short, these entreaties, and these offers, with a degree of meekness and submission, at which impartial men who were privy to my conduct were almost offended; and some of them were inclined to think, that at length my heart was subdued, or my understanding had given way, under the excess of misfortune.

They were mistaken; my conduct at this juncture differed not from that which I had observed on every other occasion of my life; I have never had recourse to measures calculated to attract the public eye, till I had tried every imaginable way of avoiding them.

And here it was not till I was left without a shadow of doubt that a plan had been formed to embitter the rest of my days, to complete the delusion of every kind of resource which yet remained to me, in sequestering me alike from my friends and my concerns, that I at length determined on a step become indispensably necessary.

Even then I listened to the scruples of a loyal subject who respects the name of his Prince, in the very abuses which his Ministers dare to make of it. Returning to *Brussels,* I had at first no idea of seeking any other retreat. Though struck with horror at the devastation of my house, with indignation at the innumerable instances of meanness and infidelity committed by the Ministerial Agents who had flocked thither to treat my effects as my person had been treated at *Paris;* I contented myself with regretting my losses, and gathering together the wrecks of my fortune. My only wish was to find some means of diverting my grief.

I had in contemplation a journey of several years: after having paid my homage at the feet of a Prince who gives such exemplary lessons of real greatness to all ether Princes, and who restores to the throne of the *Caesars*[9] a degree of lustre with which it is long since any throne has been graced; my intention was to travel into *Italy,* to try to forget in the study of the monuments of past ages, what I have suffered in the present.

This indirect method of acting in conformity to the views of the *French* Ministry was not however allowed me. I was informed by some faithful friend, that not to have piqued myself on an obedience perfectly literal, was with them no venial offence; and that by ambuscades prepared on my way, the road to *Italy* would, to me, infallibly become the road back to the *Bastille.*

As I received this intelligence from the same hand which had forewarned me of the *first Lettre-de-cachet* (for such warning I had received, though I had refused to listen to it) I thought it not prudent to brave a second. Between these Ministerial boons and me I have placed a barrier too wide for them to clear. My real protectors, those who have contributed to my safety will doubtless not to be displeased that I have taken effectual precautions to preserve the fruit of their kindness. If there are others who consider those precautions with resentment, by that very resentment they prove their necessity.

I would ask now of all honest and impartial men, What could I have done, which I have not done? What have I done, which I have not been obliged to do?

Let them deign to reflect a moment on the circumstances which have accompanied and followed the restitution of my liberty. What! to the order for my departure from *Paris*, where I had business of the last emergency, subjoin another, prohibiting me from going to *Brussels*, where concerns not less important demanded my presence! The only answer to the prayers, the offers, the very humiliations, by which I hoped to obtain a dispensation from one of those two injunctions, is a third, condemning me, after a state of inactivity, a suspension of existence, of two years duration, to continue to vegetate in the gloomy recess of an obscure borough, in irksome and fatal indolence. These are the favours, the bounties, that succeed to an oppression unprecedented in all its circumstances!

What could be the object of them? Was it to punish me? Alas for what! What was my crime? Had they ever told me? Did they even then tell me? The justice they had at length so reluctantly rendered me, sufficiently proved my innocence. Who will believe, that if they could have conjured up the shadow of a pretence for loading me with perpetual chains, they would have broken those to which they had defined me without any pretence? A malefactor convicted and condemned may indeed receive as a favour the mitigation of his punishment: but an innocent.———

Was it my duty to consider this caprice of the Ministry as a mark of paternal attention? They certainly did not affect to treat me as those are treated, who having long been deprived of sustenance, are become voracious in their appetite. It is by slow degrees that a skillful Physician prescribes to such patients that nourishment in which too sudden and liberal an indulgence might expose them to suffocation. In all probability it was not too sudden effect of too free an air that was apprehended on my account; it was not to render the regimen of liberty more salutary to me, that they had the delicacy to restore me to it only by imperceptible gradations.

If this political diet had an object it was not to me that they meant to spare the dangers of it. What it was really designed to prevent, was the explosion of those sighs which had been accumulating during two twelve months of despair; it was the aspirations of a heart tortured during that period with such cool barbarity, with so composed a neglect of every thing that was just: it was my well-grounded complaint against a species of violence which has cut off two years of my life; against those outrages, of which the effects will curtail the remainder of it; against a sort of treatment which ever has been, and perhaps ever will be, without example, even at the *Bastille*. (15) This is what they dreaded.

But, not to have made of this precaution a new outrage, an additional iniquity, it was at least necessary to have reconciled, it with the arrangement of my personal affairs, with the care of my domestic concerns. I was suing neither for pension, nor indemnity, nor appointment; I solicited nothing but permission to collect the fragments of my property, wantonly attacked, and still more wantonly dissipated. Without this permission; pillaged by the substitutes of the *French* Ministry, of the *French* Police; ruined by a perfidious Agent; unable to recover the arrears due to me, to remedy past, or prevent future depredations; how was I to have subsisted at *Rethel Mazarine?* Are these *Lettres de Cachet,* then, Letters of exchange?

It has been publickly intimated, that when I was put to the final test rewards were held out to me; that, if I had endured with resignation this last act of my martyrdom, coronets were preparing for me; but that I had rejected all with disdain, preferring the blind expectation of revenge to the peaceable enjoyment of those benefactions which would have been a full indemnity for my misfortunes.

Nothing can be more false. The only recompence which was announced to me was the chance of *learning one day or other, after being for a long time very obedient,* THE TRUE CAUSE OF MY CONFINEMENT. It was by a man in favour that this allurement was offered to me. A man in place contented himself with saying, *If you wish to live here,* TRY TO BE FORGOTTEN.

I judged it more easy, more safe, more necessary, to try to make my escape: but I once more declare; obsequious even in my apparent disobedience; still cherishing, and revering, the bands from which however those of the *Bastille* had but too fully absolved me; it was in the vicinage of my country, it was in a territory which (if I may so express myself) is a continuation of it, that I should have been content to seek a retreat, if this could have been insured me; and nothing but the excess of prevarication, and of danger, could have driven me back to the inaccessible asylum where I now am, and which I ought never to have quitted.

Those who are alarmed, perhaps not without cause, at the retreat and the independence which I now enjoy, will not fail to arm themselves with the only specious pretext which could serve the purposes of their malignity. They will accuse me of *ingratitude* and *revolt:* they will say, that if no *State crime* is to be found in my past conduct, the choice of my present asylum is one: they will paint as a criminal escape the effort which they have rendered indispensable: they will produce, as a proof of the justness those prepossessions which they opposed to the Restitution of my liberty, the use which they have forced me to make of it, and, the exercise of a faculty which, they will say, *it was in their power* to withhold from me.

That it was in their power to withhold it, is not to be doubted. Men possessed of force have it always in their option to retain, without limitation of time, what they have seized without colour of right: nothing is more dear. But that is not the point in agitation.

The question is only, on the one hand, whether, because a groundless captivity has not been an endless one too, I ought blindly to have submitted to the continuation of that rigour which originated in iniquity; and on the other hand, whether having estimated the validity of a prohibition repugnant to reason and justice, and in which it is impossible to suppose the King had any participation, I could have thought myself secure, any where else but in England, against that Ministerial despotism which had not respected even its own solemn protection?

The engagement, totally useless, but very authentic, which was signed in the name of the Count de Maurepas, who no longer exists, by the Count de Vergennes, who is still in existence, must not be forgotten: by this engagement, as hath been seen above, *the safety of my person* was guaranteed, not, as is pretended, *for a limited time*, but for ever, and without any restriction, even implied, than that, with which most assuredly I have not failed in my compliance, of continuing *to respect the King, Religion, and the State.*

Has the King been left unapprised of this basis of my security in his dominions? Or rather, in traducing me to him in order to destroy the esteem with which he honoured me[10], in order to determine him to that rigour to which the truth would certainly not have induced him, have they persuaded him that this barrier ought to be no obstacle to that rigour? Of this I know nothing.

What I do know is, that with my protection and my innocence, under a mild and an equitable reign, I have been treated, during two years, not as a person accused, pre-admonished of some offence for against such a man an action is commenced; he is informed of the accusation on which it is grounded; he is allowed to make his defence; but as a delinquent convicted of *High Treason*, with every concomitant. aggravation. Now, the *parole* of the Ministers of *France*, and the rectitude of my conduct, having failed me as guarantee: for the past, when their vindictive perfidy; was left without a pretext; what had I to expect in future, while I remained in the vicinity of *France*, after having, by a measure lawful indeed, and necessary, but contrary to their will, furnished, according to the rules of their implacable despotism, a specious pretext for some further oppression? I could not flatter myself that I should be less reprehensible: could I expect that they would become more religiously scrupulous?

Circumstanced as I then was, had I a free choice of my retreat? Could, I or ought I to have hesitated between the *Bastille s*and *Great Britain*? After having quitted without disgrace, perhaps with glory, this generous Nation, might I not without remorse come back to implore its protection[11]?

---

* In order to judge fairly of my return, it is necessary, after this, to read p. 521 of the 3d vol. of *Annales Politiques*, &c.

SECTION II

My Confinement had no just motive

FAIRLY acquitted of the charge of ingratitude or revolt in the use I have made of the liberty restored to me, I think I ought not to suffer a shadow of doubt to subsist with regard to the causes, which deprived me of it, or rather with regard to the real fact, which is, that there has been no cause which could be rationally assigned for the abuse of power, of which that privation has been the result. A summary discussion of this mailer is what I owe to myself, to my friends, to the confidence of those honest men, who, judging of my disposition by their own, have, on the sole presumption of my innocence, constantly engaged in my defence. To them I must demonstrate, that in this prepossession they have not been mistaken.

My reputation has been too long consigned to the fury of my enemies, who were then under no apprehensions of being refuted; and to the licentiousness of news-writers, justified, it is true, by the parade and the rigour of my imprisonment. How indeed could they imagine, that under a government not absolutely atrocious, and particularly under a King whose good designs are sufficiently evident, a degree of treatment so severe should be without an adequate cause?

A foreign Minister, who interested himself warmly in my behalf, as well from his own inclination, as by the special command of his sovereign, told me, at the time of my release, that no *State-Affair* had ever been more gravely discussed than mine was; and that in spite of his propensity to believe me innocent, he had concluded, from the manner in which he was silenced whenever he renewed his solicitations, that I was guilty of some treasonable offence, of which it was a mark of great lenity in government not to precipitate the chastisement.

All those, indeed, who made any efforts in my favour, found a like reception. At one time a chilling silence; at another, some tokens of pity and regret, now encomiums, even, which seemed to, indicate a friendly disposition towards me rendered ineffectual by causes exceedingly terrible; then half-words, which left a boundless and very melancholy scope to the imagination, on the enormity of the offence, and on the duration as well as justice of the punishment;—— this is what my friends experienced from men in place; from those, at least, to whom it could not be supposed the real motives of my confinement were unknown.

It is inconceivable, I confess, not only that the object of a system of intrigue like this, should in the issue prove absolutely innocent; but that he should never have been even arraigned: it is no less so, that in giving up his person to such treatment as crimes of the greatest magnitude, established on the clearest evidence, would hardly have justified, they should with an unfeeling disregard sacrifice his honour likewise to public wantonness and malignity; that they should authorize that malignity to consider, to give out, as a proof of his delinquency, the iniquitous rigour with which he was overwhelmed; that the authors of those perfidious insinuations should be those very men who best knew the iniquity, and the danger of them; in a word, that this danger and this iniquity should constitute a part of their vindictive schemes, of the selfish plan to which they meant to render these injurious falsehoods subservient.

It is inconceivable that a Ministry capable of cruelties so refined, so uniformly persevered in, and of such profound hypocrisy, should exist; that men engaged, or supposed to be engaged, in the most important public affairs, should find time to concert so scandalous an imposition; that they should thus colleague to deceive at once the Prince who honours them with his confidence, and the Public who are witnesses of their conduct; that they should enter into a confederacy to effect, by such machinations, the destruction—of whom? Of a private individual, an irreproachable character, whose only fault has been have too tenderly loved his country, and to have had too implicit a confidence in their plighted word. This, however, is a fact no less true than astonishing.

I know not (I must say it again) what may have been told to the King; what calumnies may have been employed to make the apparent necessity of crushing me, as if by a thunder-clap, preponderate in his mind against the pleasure he appeared to take in reading my works, and the propensity he had to protect me. Not a word of this has ever been communicated to me: during my twenty months confinement, I have never undergone the shadow of an interrogatory, not the least appearance of an examination. And here, in the face of all *Europe,* I solemnly defy the *French* Ministers to produce one single act, to prove that in their proceedings against me they have regarded the least formality.

My enlargement, as hath already been shewn, was accompanied with the same mystery: in the order of exile the same silence has been observed: so that I know not precisely again of what to justify myself since I am absolutely ignorant of what they might have laid to my charge.

This very silence, observed towards a man who was languishing under every species of aggravated cruelty, in which a full and striking conviction is implied, bespeaks, doubtless, a strong prepossession in his favour. It is what all laws universally proscribe; what is no where allowed but at the *Bastille;* and what perhaps, even there, except in my case alone, they have never dared to venture upon. The nullity or the falsehood of accusation would need no other proof.

But what is more, what will effectually remove the last degree of doubt, is, that I have been incessantly told at the *Bastille,* that my confinement originated in the immediate and direct will of the King; that I was not a man so obscure, so insignificant, that such a stroke of authority would have been hazarded against me without his consent. This is the sacred barrier that has been confidently opposed to my endeavours to attain, if not the full discovery, at least a partial glimpse, of the ground, so cautiously concealed, of my imprisonment. It is, then, on some kind of delinquency, on some express and positive accusation, that this will, this consent, have been founded.

Ah, ye audacious calumniators! whose attempt to rob me of the esteem of that Protector whom nature and providence had given me, might have prevailed, it is before his footstool that I summon you: it is in the presence of Him whose honest and liberal soul you have abused, that I impeach you. If you have said anything to him, which could for a moment bring in question my loyalty to his person, my devotion to his interests, my horror for every kind of intrigue in general, and especially for such as might have had an opposite tendency; I declare to you in formal terms, that every word you have uttered has been a lye.

Do not flatter yourselves that you will be able to shrink from my representations, under the veil, so often profaned, of respect due to *Secrets of State:* do not deceive yourselves in the vain hope that this will conceal the springs of your fraudulent despotism, as the *Bastille* conceals its operations. No; I will pursue you into that asylum which you pollute: I will there resound, without ceasing, these words, so terrible to you, and so which perhaps the equitable Monarch, in whose presence I address them to you, will not be insensible: "You have basely imposed upon him. My conduct and my writings have always been incorrupt as my heart."

You have suffered it to be said, to be affirmed, to be printed all the public papers, "That I had composed and communicated Memoirs calculated to draw embarrassing claims upon France, or at least to awaken the desire of asserting them." This is the rumour which I found to have most generally obtained, on my resurrection from my grave: this is the opprobrium to which you had devoted my ashes, if, in spite of your endeavors, an all-powerful hand had not snatched me out of it.

Perhaps your view in opposing yourselves to my return to Brussels, was still to confirm, to give additional credit to that falsehood, so criminal, and so absurd. Perhaps, after having had the cunning to render it probable in the eyes of those whom you wished to deceive, you have had that too of retarding an *éclaircissement* between the two Sovereigns whom it concerned, and of preventing an explanation by which I should have been justified.

Nay, perhaps dreading the protection with which I was honored by the august and virtuous Princess[12] who is the band of their union, you have forged this calumny merely to reduce her to silence when my affair should be the object of discussion. Consort of the one, and sister of the other, till facts were cleared up, she must have been cautious of appearing to interest herself for a man suspected of having failed of his duty alike towards them both: and how were those facts to be cleared, when on the delicate subject, on which you had raised suspicions, it was so easy to elude an *éclaircissement*.

Your interest, however, will not enable you to stifle this my solemn protestation. Exclusively limited in my literary toils, I have indulged myself in no other political speculations whatever, but those I have published in the *Annals:* and, for the sake of refuting the falsehood which you have either invented, or tolerated, I here presume to invoke that august Sovereign whose name is called in question. Far from giving myself up to that unaccountable madness which would have disposed me to foretell and to justify the dismemberment of *France,* it is in her bosom that with unceasing views I have been preparing myself a retreat: (16) it is on her prosperity that I have perpetually rested the dependence of my own, till the very moment in which you have requited the tenderest attachment with torments scarcely reserved for her most implacable enemies; till that moment, of all her children none has been more affectionately obedient, of all her subjects none more scrupulously faithful.

If I had ever conceived the idea of sentiment different from those I here unfold, some traces of it must doubtless still exist. Ah! dare then to disclose them; bring forth into open day: ransack your *bureaux;* put in motion the priviledged spies whose clandestine zeal you have so dearly paid. If at length I am found guilty, the boldness of my denial will ultimately excite, in those with whom the proofs of my perfidy are deposited, a degree of indignation proportioned to the contempt with which my original treachery would have inspired them in the beginning: they will be eager to assist you in bringing to confusion an hypocritical impostor, who should dare to flatter himself that he could impose on your indulgence, who should so strenuously endeavour to reconcile the appearance of virtue with the stratagems of inquiry. There is neither *State-concern,* nor *State-secret,* which can possibly be an obstacle to discoveries that would be so dear to you.

But far, very far, am I from fearing them! My conduct, as my works in general, without the least exception, has constantly borne the stamp of one uniform sentiment; I mean, that of a patriotic enthusiasm, a delicacy on this point, carried to the extreme. Here, my tongue, my pen, and my heart have been invariably in union. Here I have left no alternative, but those of refuting me upon facts, of acknowledging how odious, how criminal have been those artifices which could for a moment render my innocence problematical.

But has my private correspondence been equally unexceptionable as my public conduct? Have I not been guilty of some internal act of imprudence, some secret indiscretion, sufficient to justify the animadversion of government? Have I not shocked some man in power, to whose rank some reparation may have been judged due? This is the last resource of my persecutors: it is also the last stroke of that fatality which has destined me to be a model of passive oppression in every possible way.

Is it not strange, after what I have suffered from the fury of Corporations, from the prevarication of men in place, that I should be obliged to vindicate myself on such an occasion as this; to give an account of every sigh which indignation has extorted from me, of all the convulsions which grief has thrown me into? I must not however decline the enumeration; both because it is necessary, and because it will complete the discovery of all those enormities, of all that cowardice, of which I have been the victim.

The only complaint, of the kind last mentioned, which has

been communicated to me, that which has been presented to me as the sole cause of my confinement, is a letter to the *Marshal de Duras*[13]. I pretend not to justify it, and its discussion would be useless: but it was a private letter, which concerned him only in his private character; a letter, which had been challenged, and even necessitated by a sort of conduct more reprehensible than the letter itself was violent; a secret letter, which I have never exposed; a letter which I have never denied to have written, because I am not capable of a lye, but which the Marshal *de Duras,* at least in public, has always denied to have received; a letter of which he constantly averred he had made no complaint; of which he had in fact made so little, that, notwithstanding my requisitions, they could not produce me the original; and which, consequently, could by no means constitute the ground of any suit or punishment whatsoever; a letter, in short, upon which my answer, when I was asked if I had written it, ought to have put Hatred to the blush, and made Vengeance drop her arms. (17)

Whatever it was, it is evident that the exposure of it could alone render it criminal; and it had not been exposed. Whatever it was, though it had even been published with as much scandal as that which accompanied my confinement, it was no *State Crime.* Whatever it was certainly it could not have justified twenty months imprisonment in the *Bastille;* with a continuance of the most atrocious treatment of which that infernal precinct had even been the theatre.

I am well aware that my readers will be curious to know the tenour of this piece, so fatal and so mysterious; and, were I sensible to the thirst of vengeance alone, I should certainly make it public. But, here again I am tenacious of my respect even for the intentions of the King: my letter no sooner appears to move his displeasure, than I abandon it; I sacrifice it to the opinion which he entertains of it, setting no higher value on this last homage, than the satisfaction of having paid it. (18)

But in the cabinet of the French Ministers there exists another letter, which has contributed, perhaps in a greater degree, than the former, to my misfortune. This, however, they have taken effectual care to keep back from the eye of the King: if, indeed, it had been said before him, it would have secured me against all I have suffered. I was never so much as once reminded of it: but, as I have not a doubt that it had much greater influence, than the other, on the resolution of the Ministry: as it is evident, that in making use of the former to irritate the mind of the King, they had the discretion to conceal from him the latter, which could only alarm and exasperate his Ministers, I am of opinion that I ought to give a place here.

This letter was dated on the morrow after that to the Marshal *de Duras:* it was addressed to M. *Le Noir,* Lieutenant of the Police, through whose hands the *Annales* regularly passed, in order to be delivered to the distributor.

It is necessary to recollect, that in March, 1770, the 59th and 60th Numbers had been successively stopped, at the solicitation of the Marshal *de Duras,* and the *Parliament of Paris.* The first suppression I had patiently submitted to: on the second, I wrote, the 9th of April, 1780, to the Marshal *de Duras,* the letter which he does not hand about, nor I neither; and on the morrow, to M. *Le Noir* that which follows.

Brussels, April 8, 1780.

"Sir,

"After having, in my letter of yesterday, given way, to an indignation well founded, I am going to make some further efforts in the name of justice and reason; though I have learnt to *my cost,* how little weight in they have in *France* against interest and intrigue. The following is a short memorial, which I entreat you to lay before the eyes of the Ministers: they will not fail to impute it, still, to my obstinacy; but I presume it should be ascribed to the goodness of my cause.

"I cannot conceive that the Marshal *de Duras* would wish to figure any longer in public. I confess, that no thing can be added to what the Count *Desgrée*[14] has told him: however, it is something to repeat it, and to remark to the Public, that the *Marshal* has obtained no satisfaction for it. It appears to me, that in his situation, he ought, of all things, to avoid making a noise in the world; and he is going to make more than he has ever done in his life.

"Be this as it may, I can only repeat to you what I have already had the honour of saying to you several times, on my aversion to be again involved in the bickerings of past times, on the ardent desire I have of being no more exposed to them; but, at the same time, on the courage with which I shall support myself under them. It will cost me my fortune; but I am accustomed to sacrifices.

"The sale of the N°s. LIX. and LX. of the *Annales* has been stopped at *Paris:* they are published and circulated in *England,* in *Holland,* in *Germany,* in the *Low Countries;* and even in *France,* by the pirates who *counterfeit* them. To suppress in *Paris* only the genuine edition, while all the others are tolerated, and even encouraged, is to do an act of injustice at once very shocking, and totally useless: it will not hinder the prohibited Numbers from finding their way into *Paris;* it will only render them more noted, more fought for, and more valuable: the desire of them will be only the more lively, and of longer continuance. I don't see what the parties concerned have to gain by it. These Numbers contain nothing censurable: far from it: the 59th might have been infinitely more severe. I do not imagine that the interests of the very ridiculous Nephew of M. de Leyrit[15] (19) have the least weight in this suppression. The only object, then, is to spare the Marshal de Duras the disagreeable circumstances of a mortifying reflection on his affair. But is that peculiar to this Number? Or rather, is it not there that it is softened, at least to the advantage of the commandant?

"When two men, destined by their birth and condition to give an example of probity in their actions, and of delicacy in their words, mutually accuse each other, in the face of all Europe of every kind of knavery, and larceny, making use of those very terms: and when they have recourse to a regular

Tribunal to obtain reparation and justice: if that Tribunal leaves the affair undecided, it commits at least one act of prevarication, and perhaps two. If one of the parties is guilty, it is scandalous, that the decree of the Court should encrease suspicions, instead of destroying them should stigmatise two innocent men, instead of acquitting them. This is all that I have said: and it is upon the judges that my reflection falls. This is all that I have said: and it is upon the judges that my reflection falls. The Public is not so indulgent: it is the Writer of *Castellan*[16] whom it points out as the man really guilty: and the supplicated suppression of the 59th Number will not reinstate him.

"As to the contents of No. LX, they are facts. The vexations of the *Parliaments;* their secret tyrannies; the support which the Members all think they owe one to the other, and in reality afford one another on occasions where they ought the least to allow themselves to confound one another on occasions where they ought the least to allow themselves to confound their legal character with their private interests:— the corruptness of the *Secretaries*[17]*;* their intrigues, their perfidies, their custom of extorting fees on both sides, are notorious matters. As authority does not deign either to punish, or repress these abuses, it is necessary at least that the certainty of not being able to screen them from public censure, should put some kind of restraint upon them; it is the interest of Government; it is the interest of those very Companies who are degraded by so many excesses.

"*Whilst I wrote from* ENGLAND, *I was exposed to none of these broils;* and I wrote things much more forcible. (20) It is however upon the plan conceived, digested, and executed in *England,* and well known in *France,* that the agreements took place between the Public in *France, the* Posts of *France,* and myself. It was in conformity to that plan the subscriptions were opened and received; that the circulation of the work was authorized; and that the King accepted the copies which I addressed immediately to him. It was not stipulated as a condition, that I should respect the cowardice of the *Marshals of France*[18]*,* if either of them should be guilty of any, or the prevarication of the Tribunals. No such terms were proposed to me; none, such should I have accepted.

"I never meant to subject myself to any Censorial power: on the contrary, I have loudly protested, I have more than once declared in print, that I would never have any other Censor than my own delicacy. I have not said one word which might subject that to be called in question. Whence then those trammels in which they take upon them to confine me.

"Repassing the sea, I have changed my situation, but not my heart: I have without reluctance sacrificed my fortune; I will never sacrifice my independence, nor the prerogatives to which a solemn obligation has entitled me. I may suffer for my passionate regard for *France,* for my confidence, in the Ministry of *France,* for my absolute devotion to my Country: I may be determined, by downright disgust, to leave off writing; but I shall never be reduced to write like a slave. Of all the indemnities due to me from the Government of *France,* that which I believe to be the least costly, and I am sure is the most useful to her, is the freedom of my pen!"

This letter I do not doubt, I never have doubted, though I have never spoken of it, as the real cause of my misfortunes: this is what has determined the Ministry of *France* to seize the opportunity of revenge. At the time of my departure from *England* they could not refuse to the firmness, the integrity of my conduct, the solemn protection of which I have spoken; and since that time they have not been able to find any pretence to violate it.

Further, I owe this justice to the memory of the Count *de Maurepas:* he was neither vindictive, nor implacable: entirely taken up in perpetuating his case, and his influence, he sought no other enjoyment. What was lively in the *Annales* amused him: what was serious, gave him no uneasiness. Perhaps he found a pleasure even, in the idea that it, was himself who had the credit of protecting me.

His agents in administration were not altogether of the same way of thinking: some of them still bore in mind the letter to the Count de *Vergennes*, and the portraits that were drawn in it: others dreaded the unreserved frankness of the *Annales*. Pickpockets, says a certain intelligent man, *shun the light of the lamps*. The great success of that work, the very respectable suffrages united in its favour the friendly zeal of all those who had nothing to fear from it, that is, of all virtuous and impartial men, had held Malevolence in chains.

But when, for the purpose of extorting the consent of the old Minister, they had the letter of the 8th of April, which was shewn only to him, and which, he might without difficulty be led to construe in a menace: when to prejudice the mind of the young King, they had the other letter of the 7th, which like wise was produced only to Him, with additions which he alone was to hear; it was easy to fabricate the Order which till then they had perhaps despaired of obtaining. It will not be doubted that the business was transacted in the manner I have here suggested, when it is considered that the letter to M. *Le Noir* is of the VIIIth of April, 1780, and the *Letter-de-cachet* of the XVIth of the same month. But from this same date another kind of inference is to be drawn. My hand yet starts at the very idea of it; and it is with equal horror, and depression of spirits, that I am going to disclose it.

The 16th of April 1780, I was not in *France*. I had it in my option never to have returned thither: and, if my blind fanaticism for my Country; if my confidence, yet more, extravagant than blind; in a promise of the *French* Ministers, joined to a thousand treacheries, of which a specimen will presently be seen, had not made me neglect intelligence but too well grounded; I never should have returned thither. The *Lettre-de-cachet*, therefore, might never have been put in force. This thunderbolt, then, was forged at a venture, without any knowledge whether it would ever produce its effect. The *French* Ministry, it seems, keep these murderous weapons in reserve[19]; they have magazines where these instruments of its vengeance are deposited; and they can peaceably wait, like the sportsman in ambush, till the game presents itself of its own accord, to receive the shot which he is ready to aim for its destruction.

Nor is this all; for they imitate the cunning of this sportsman no less with respect to the preliminaries than to the object. A variety of perfidious tricks, some of them more cowardly than others, have been successively multiplied to conceal from me the snare which had been just laid in my way. Is not even the currency restored to the *Annales* in their distribution, immediately after the 16th of April, one of the most criminal kind!

What! continue to circulate in public, under guarantee of the Royal authority, a work, of which the Author has been secretly proscribed, and devoted by the Ministers to that disgrace, to that severity, which are reserved for the enemies of the King and the State! continue to receive it in order to deliver it to the King, and actually deliver it to him; affect to applaud the marks of satisfaction with which he did not cease to honour it; and take special care that I should be acquainted with this.

The same engine by which the news of an approbation so flattering was conveyed to me, was employed to entice me to *Paris*. That spy; under the mask of a friend, who had been pensioned by the Police, at my expense, for five years past to penetrate into my secrets, having learnt that I was not unacquainted with this circumstance laboured incessantly to dissipate the terror with which it had inspired me, by this consideration, that they would not have restored liberty to the *Annales,* if they had wished to deprive the Author, of that of his person; and that I might go into France, without any apprehensions, as my works were so favourably received at *Versailles.* Thus the sacred name of the King was made use of to facilitate the success of an iniquity, of which that very name was to be the instrument.

This iniquity was not perpetrated till the end of six months; but at the end of six years, of twenty, the *Lettre-de-cachet* which authorised it, would have had the same efficacy. I was devoted, then, for the rest of my life, to undergo, at some time or other, the stab of this poignard ; and recompence for so many exertions and sacrifices, permission to die there in peace, I should have found no gates open to receive me but the *Bastille*, no other sepulchre but its dungeons!

After these reflections, what, in God's name, can we style the Lettre-de-cachet of the 16th of April 1780! How describe that eagerness to fabricate it, and that patience in waiting the moment of its execution!

Let it now be considered, that an imprisonment thus instated, thus prepared and thus consummated, has lasted near two years; that it has done me an injury, almost equally irreparable, in my property, and in my health: that, if it has not totally ruined me in my civil capacity, and closed my life at an untimely period, I owe this to a peculiar favour of Providence, which, having apparently destined me to the talk I am now performing, I mean, making public the horrors of the Bastille, has endued me with an organisation expressly calculated to support them.

If it is to the Marshal *de Duras* that so ample a satisfaction has been thought due, one should hardly be able to forbear repeating what was said on this occasion by one of the greatest monarchs in Europe: *"This Monsieur de Duras then must be a very great Personage!"*

Examples on this subject would amount to nothing: in a matter where all is caprice and despotism; authorities and comparisons are very useless. I cannot however help citing one.

Among the numberless *Imbastillements*, which have been designed as a satisfaction to powerful Personages, may be reckoned that of *La Beaumelle*[BST]. This writer, more than

---

[BST] Linguet's version is not accurate. Laurent Anglivielle de la Beaumelle (1727-1773) was a writer who had a long-running feud with Voltaire. His first stay in the Bastille came in 1753, after he'd inserted a critique of the Orleans family in an edition of Voltaire's *Siècle de Louis XIV*. Next, it was a book on Mme. De Montespan, one of Louis XIV's mistresses, that got him locked up, 1756-1757, in part because he was accused of having stolen the originals of some of the source material. However, says one author, "It cannot be doubted that Voltaire and his numerous partisans were the principle instigators of these persecutions" - a reminder that the

indiscreet, had dared to insert, in his Memoirs of Madame *de Maintenon,* the following phrase: *"The Court of Vienna, long accused* of *keeping in pay, people ready to administer poison,....."* The offence was certainly henious, as well as public: the punishment might therefore justly be severe, and reparation exemplary.

However, *five months* in the *Bastille* appeared sufficient. *La Beaumelle* found an effectual protection in the generosity of the very Court which he had insulted: it was at the solicitation of that Court that he was enlarged–and without being exiled.

However mighty the Marshal *de Duras,* as a man of arms; however accomplished the Marshal *de Duras* as a man of letters; however refined the Marshal *de Duras* as a man of wit; however great the Marshal *de Duras* as an *Academician;* not notwithstanding all these titles, it is not probable that he has appeared to the *French* Ministry, himself, all alone, a personage more important than the House of *Austria* all together. However violent, my six unknown lines to the Marshal *de Duras* may be supposed, it cannot be imagined they were comparable to the public calumniation, equally atrocious as false, in the romance just mentioned.

If then the Marshal *de Duras* had condescended to serve as Sponsor to the *Lettre-de-cachet* against me in the time of its infancy, it is clear that I am not to impute to him the guilt of its protracted existence: he could not have asked, nor would they have offered him, so tedious an atonement. (21) If it has not been believed that this atonement was demanded by a terrestrial divinity somewhat, more respectable, it is not the fault of that indiscretion or rather that malignity, which was everywhere busied in seeking matter of censure against me, and of exculpation in favour of the *French* Ministry. That malignity has not been contented with calling in question the name of a single sovereign on my account. After having given out my pretended connection with one, as the motive of the iniquity of the 27th of September 1780, they have endeavored

---

'Enlightened' factions of the time did not oppose the Bastille's use when it suited them. Chéron (Web); *Mémoires de Linguet,* 186.

to make another a direct accomplice in it. It has been circulated abroad, that the *Lettre-de-cachet* had been granted at the instance of his *Prussian* Majesty[20]. The rumour was spread, and still subsists, that that Monarch, piqued at the Epistle to M. *Alembert*[*21] and, at the particulars which I thought proper, to publish of the famous affair of the *Miller*[†22], and further stimulated by the entreaties of the little *Platos* of *Paris*[23], had been earnest at *Versailles*, in solliciting my imprisonment; that the *French* Ministry could not refuse this mark of condescension to a Philosopher of such importance; and that the gates of my prison could not possibly be opened without the consent of him by whose order they had been shut.

But is it probable, that a Legislator so equitable, so, beneficent in his own dominions, would have sunk so low as to solicit an act of injustice and oppression, on his behalf in the dominions of another? Is it probable, that having lately done the Author of the *Annals* the honour of adopting his very expressions in one of his laws,[*24] he would have indulged himself in a caprice of this kind against that same writer, who had never offended him? Is it probable, besides, that *Versailles* would have thought she owed so cruel an homage to *Potzdam*; that they would have dared to propose to the King of *France* to become an instrument of vengeance to the King of *Prussia?* With regard to such public offence as tend to blast the honour of a Crown, like that of *La Beaumelle*, of whom I have just now spoken, Princes may undoubtedly render each other the service of repressing them, all though not personally interested but in all other respects they carry their jealousy of power so high, as to protect, and that sometimes to the prejudice of public order, even persons who are criminal. How is it possible then to suspect them of acting in concert to proscribe one who was innocent?

In short, what completes the justification of his *Prussian* Majesty, and clearly proves that I have not been the *Callisthenes*[25] of this *Alexander* of the North, is the date of the *Letter-de-cachet* in question. The 16th of April, 1780 is

---

* See *Annales Politiques, &c* Vol. ix. P. 79.

† Ibid. p. 4, &c.

* See the *Annales*, Vol; vii. p. 434-

considerably prior to the pretended wrongs with which they would have connected it. It is evident then, that that Prince has not tarnished his philosophical career, in persecuting with such animosity a writer who has not indeed courted his favour, but from whom he certainly could not withhold his esteem.

The particulars of the treatment I underwent, and the very duration of my imprisonment, are so many additional proofs that he took no part in the affair. If he had been the real author of it, would not the loss of my liberty have appeared to him an ample satisfaction? Would he have required of the Ministers of *Versailles* those refinements of revenge of which I am presently to treat? Or could they have mistaken him so far, so grossly insulted him, as to mean by such measures to conciliate his good will? Far from wishing to protract my distress would not his generosity have urged him to imitate the example of the Court of *Vienna* towards *La Beaumelle?* Having infinitely less cause of complaint, would he have given way to a greater degree of implacability? Would we have prescribed for a Frenchman, at the *Bastille,* those severities which one of his own subjects, really criminal, would not have had to fear at *Spandau?*

It is very astonishing that the names of two Princes so illustrious should have been thus blended with the misfortunes of a private individual; of him, who, on account of his personal simplicity, his dislike to all sorts of parade, his abhorrence of every kind of intrigue, his indifference to fortune and every ambitious pursuit, ought perhaps, of all men who cultivate literature, to have been the least exposed to the dangers attending the honour of being known to Sovereigns: but it is at, least equally evident, that neither of those whom I have here mentioned could possibly have contributed to what I have undergone. My imprisonment has no more owed its origin, or its duration, to the pretended requisitions sent from *Berlin,* than to the pretended communications dispatched to *Vienna.*

What then has been the motive, the object of this duration? That indeed has not been concealed from me: it is the only mark of confidence ever shown me at the *Bastille,* the only answer with which my supplications have been honoured.

At the expiration of a fortnight I was plainly told that the Marshal *of Duras* was now quite out of the question. If not the M. *de Duras,* pray; what is it then?--Oh, THEY are afraid that you will seek opportunities of revenge: the doors would presently be opened to you, if THEY were sure that you would not *flourish* away against them. For in speaking to me of the Deities of this *Tartarus* they always made use of the collective word THEY. This is what was constantly told me during *Twenty months,* and what the public knew very well without my telling them.

Putting himself now in MY place, let the reader judge with what terror, with what heavy indignation, these cowardly confessions must have filled my soul. It was, then, a future and uncertain *edict* which determined my present servitude! After I had been sacrificed to vindictive injustice, its effects were perpetuated against me merely for the tranquility of my oppressors! According to their political ritual I ought to have been detained so long as I was to be *dreaded;* that is, till my soul should have been debased, or my organs deranged, or at least my feeble talents destroyed by the frigidity of age, and the convulsions of despair. What an unacountable destiny! When the point in debate was, to rob me of my civil establishment, in complaisance to a band of *enrobed* assassins, an *Advocate general,* their accomplice, devoid of all shame, said in open court, in full audience, that I could not possibly be left in possession of it, because of the troubles *I should not fail* ONE DAY[*] *to excite,* in--I know not what order of men: and here, where my person was to be disposed of, it was coldly consigned to endless slavery, on account of the resentment which *I should not fail* ONE DAY *to entertain!*

Thus, ever peaceable in reality, and formidable in idea; always blameless at the present, and criminal in the future; it is for the hereafter that I have been punished. My enemies have never been able to excuse their iniquities but by presages yet more iniquitous. They have always assigned, as a motive for their cruelties of today my *infallible* resentment of

---

[*] See *Appel a la Posterité,* page 35

tomorrow! They have never vouchsafed to make the trial whether it was not their presages, dictated by a stupid degree of timidity, or a cunning kind of hatred, that were void of foundation.

Here, a very fair opportunity, doubtless, presented itself. The uncorrupt and feeling heart of the King was moved at the remembrance of my distress. Whilst intrigue was bustling to dazzle his integrity, and calumny loquacious to mislead it; it was watchful, it was eloquent in my favour: he was sensible that the punishment of those faults, whatever they might be, of which he at that time believed me guilty, ought not to be eternal. A secret preposition, in favour of my innocence, had perhaps, even before this rendered the virulence of his Counselors suspicious: and, in spite of their efforts, he pronounced the all powerful *Surge* & *ambula*[26], which put an end to my misfortunes.

Was not this the moment, if reason at least, for want of justice, if an enlightened policy had had any effect on the mind of the Ministers, to try what indulgence might have had upon mine; upon that untamable spirit, whose extravagant sallies they pretended to have been obliged to check by so exemplary a punishment? I have unceasingly repeated, in the thousand and one memorials which I breathed in sighs from the depths of the *Bastille,* that I knew my Country only by her rigours; and that I adored her. What would have been my idolatry, at that juncture when, renouncing every unjust prejudice, every cruel caprice, her sons should have met me with open arms; when to those sentiments, which her severities had not changed, I could have added that of gratitude for the earnest of one single act of kindness[*]; when,

---

[*] These words require an explanation that I cannot place amongst the Notes: it concerns me so nearly, that I would not have it go unnoticed.

Amongst the innumerable absurdities and falsehoods of which my misfortunes, as usual, have rendered me the object one has gone abroad, which I cannot pass by with neglect: it has been said, it has been written, it has been printed, that the claims of the *French* Ministry upon me were so much the stronger, as I had received from them *a pension of two thousand crowns.*

reinstated in the common privileges of the family, I might

I am obliged to declare, that there never was a more impudent falsehood. It is unaccountable that it should have been hazarded, at any time posterior to the 27th of September, 1780, after what I had said in the preceding August, N°. LIX. p. *296* in the *Annales:*
"There is only one of the Kings of Europe towards whom respect, attachment, and fidelity, on my part, can be considered as duties; one alone, from whom I MIGHT HAVE accepted benefactions without a blush, and without a scruple. Now, even of Him, I never asked, I never will ask anything but justice."

It is immaterial here what was the answer made to this demand: but it is clear that the man who held this language publickly, in a printed work, was not *pensioned*.

The only marks of attention which I have received from the *French* Ministry during my life have been three *Lettres-de-cachet*, one for the *Bastille*, and two of *Exile;* of which the first was my punishment for having as *Counsel* defended M. *de Bellegarde,* who was at first solemnly condemned as guilty, and three years after, as solemnly acknowledged innocent.

The other affairs which I have treated, either as a Civilian, or merely as a Man of Letters, have not all been found worthy of such flattering distinctions: but there is not one of them, of which the success, so far as it respected me, was not embittered by the ingratitude of the Clients whom I saved, the prevarications of the Tribunals which I compelled to be just, the stupidity nor the corruption of the men in place whom I unmasked. It cannot be imputed to self-sufficiency, when I declare that neither the Bar, nor the Republic of Letters, have produced a man whose life has been interspersed with anecdotes more incredible of this kind, from the Defence of the *Duc d'Aiguillon,* down to my Reflections on that of M. *de Lally.*

I will dare to go further, even though the charge of self-sufficiency should be brought against me, and the old cry of *egotism* revived: There has not been a writer whose zeal was more pure, whose soul more inaccessible to intrigue and personal influence, whose talent more exclusively devoted to the protection of justice, and the manifestation of truth: and this is sufficiently evident from the fruits they have yielded me.

Having spoken of the exile occasioned by the defence of M. *de Bellegarde,* I must render due homage to the generosity shewn by the Marshal *de Biron* on that occasion. He was chief of the Council of War which the *Lettre-de-cachet* seemed to avenge: he was extremely active in accelerating its revocation; and on my return, a very polite, a very flattering reception was the balm he poured into my wound.

Of Gallic Knights even such is the renown.

But this is apparently not the character or the *Literary* Knights, nor of the *Academic* Marshals.

have said to myself: I have hitherto suffered from vexatious prejudices; let us endeavour to destroy them. I have been accused of obstinacy, and too much vehemence of temper; let us carry meekness and patience even to the extreme: let us try to dissipate fear, disarm hatred, and take away every pretext of uneasiness.

Rising from my sepulcher, my first movements tended to confirm these dispositions. Like another *Lazarus,* disencumbered of the grave-clothes which for twenty months had intercepted every motion of my tongue, and my heart, it was sensibility, it was the love of peace, it was *gratitude* that I announced. For five whole weeks I have not ceased to tender these cowardly and implacable despots, my hands yet bleeding from the chains with which they had so long been loaded. I asked of them only the favour to try me, and I was not able to obtain it! they did not dare to believe my words were sincere. Unworthy to form a judgement of my heart, they imagined their *Lettres-de-cachet* a more powerful check than my delicacy: and while the enjoyment of a state of freedom, henceforward, inviolably secured to me, is hardly a consolation for the price it cost me, they are congratulating themselves perhaps on the sagacity which enabled them to foretell the use *I should not fail* to make of it.

Away with these unreasonable retrospects and regrets! Having been refused permission to convince the *French* Ministry of my resigned disposition, let us make use of the faculty they have forced me to assume, to unmask their injustice, and divulge their barbarity. The former is already sufficiently obvious: let us proceed to the detail of the latter; and, if on the perusal of these Memoirs, some readers are tempted to say that no oppression has ever been upbraided with equal energy, let us force them in like manner to confess that none has ever been attended with equal cruelty.

NOTES.

N. B. *The Reader is requested not to proceed to the Notes, till after having read, and, if possible, paused a little upon the Text.*

(1) PAGE 2. *At the avenues of these abysses.]* In *France* all the strongholds in general may at pleasure be converted into so many *Bastilles:* there is not one of these ramparts, apparently raised against the enemies of the State, which may not at any juncture of ministerial caprice be made the grave of her children. However, there are only about twenty castles that have this special and fixed destination; as, the *Bastille* and *Vincennes*, at the gates of *Paris; Pierre en Cise*, at *Lyons;* the *Isles Ste. Marguerite*, in *Provence;* the *Mont St Michel*, in *Normandy;* the *Château du Taureau* in *Brittany;* that of *Saumur*, in *Anjou;* that of *Ham*, in *Picardy, &c. &c. &c.* And all these are filled with *Prisoners of State;* in all of them the regimen of the *Bastille* is followed; and all of these have their *Suttling Governors*(*), turn-keys of the Etat-Major, *Garrison, Engineers,* &c.

The consideration of this enormous expence has given some Ministers, (among others, Mr. *Necker*[1], as it is said) a faint inclination to a reform: if this should ever be effected, it would be very shameful that it had no other motive. A few days ago, on this occasion, one of the youngest and most eloquent Orators in England, said with indignation, *Suppress the Bastille through* OECONOMY!

(2) Page 2. *A Condé.]* There is an anecdote in the Memoirs of *Sully*, little attended to perhaps by most readers, which this name brings to my mind, and to which I cannot refuse a place here[2]. Henry the Fourth, in spite of his old age and his virtues, had, in his latter days given way to a passion equally shameful and ridiculous: he was in love with the Princess of

---

* See Part II. The 83rd and following pages.

Condé, his nephew's wife. He had married her to him, in hopes that being young, dissipated, and avaricious, he might possibly by pleasures, and by money, be blinded to his wife's conduct. No such thing: the young Prince, wanted neither to amuse, nor enrich himself: he took his wife to *Brussels*, without saying a word of it to anybody. This flight could not but be approved by all people of probity; in the Council of the King, it was treated as an *Affair of State*. All the Ministers, first one, and then another, gave their opinions gravely on the means of bringing back to the arms of the King, with all possible haste, a Mistress whom the disobliging Husband had dared to take away from him. Some of them declared *for war;* and when it came to the turn of the *Duc de Sully*, he began his opinion in these words: *if you had left the matter to me three months ago, I would have had your man in the* Bastille, *or I'd have answered for it at my peril*†.

It was in *full Counsel* that this language was held! he who held it was one of the most virtuous Ministers that *France* ever had; he against whom it was held, was a *Prince of the Blood;* and the crime of this *Prince of the Blood*, adjudged worthy of the *Bastille*, was that of having a pretty wife, and not chusing that she should be the mistress of his uncle.

Readers, reflect!

(3) Page 4. *Let his description be compared with mine.*] I do not place in the class of Memoirs to be consulted on the detail of this *Trophonius's cave*[3], a certain history of the *French Inquisition*, written by *Constantine de Renneville*[BST]. This book, now become

---

† I quote from memory: I may be mistaken in a word or two; but I am sure I am not mistaken on the fact, nor in the phrase.

[BST] It should be noted that the most famous first-hand accounts of the Bastille – Renneville's, Latude's and Linguet's - are all more or less subject to question. Latude (Danry) lied about his very name. Linguet was at the least prone to exaggeration. Constantine de Renneville's *L'Inquisition Française* includes some dubious passages – notably the one Linguet refers to – and has been questioned by other writers. But many of his references to prisoners and others have been verified, as have a number of his observations on the Bastille itself. I have frequently used Albert Savine's richly annotated version as a source here.

scarce, and dear on account of its scarcity, contains nothing interesting, or even true, but the title. It is a medley of disgusting nonsense, and absurd fables.

We read there, for instance, that a prisoner having been shut up in the subterranean dungeons of one of the towers; tore up *with his hands* so many of the foundation stones, that he made the tower shake; and that the affrighted Governor was forced to lodge this new *Samson* in the most superb apartment of the castle in order to prevent its fall. The author of this tale did not know, then, that the walls of the *Bastille*, even in their thinnest parts, are at least *twelve feet* thick, and in others, even thirty, forty, or fifty; that they are of the finest freestone, and consequently as solid as the hearts of the keepers are relentless. Besides, *Renneville* speaks only of the tortures inflicted on the body. It is true, that these are not spared in this place, where every method of rendering existence insupportable is put in practice: but it is not on this resource that the interrogators of the *order of St. Louis*[BST], who are charged with the barbarous office, place their chief dependence: it is the soul that they torture; and that is infinitely more ingenious.

(4) Page 5. *Apparently consecrated to justice.*] This officer is the *Lieutenant General of the Police*. He is the real administrator of the *Bastille*, the Governor in chief of that castle: it is through him that all orders pass: he has no superior in that district, but the direct Minister for the department of *Paris*.

This association of the *Robe* with the *Sword*[4], of a Magistrate with armed Mercenaries, for the purpose of completing an oppression which the Laws proscribe, and which the *Robe*, which the *Magistracy* profess to hold in abhorrence, is an inconsistency, of which no instance is to be found but in *France*. Nor is it to alleviate this oppression that the administration of it is confided to a *Master of the Requests*[5]: it is to render it in a manner legitimate, or however legal if it were possible.

[BST] The Royal and Military Order of St. Louis was founded by Louis XIV in 1693. The king was its grand master. Membership was subject to a number of conditions, including twenty five years of service to the king. (Cheruel, II, 1125). No other author consulted here confirms Linguet's assertion, which seems questionable, .that it was worn by Bastille staff.

The troops of the *general Farm*[6], the Soldiers of the Finance, in *France* have a right to perform civil and juridical acts, to draw up verbal processes; to make those whom they arrest, and whom they search, undergo necessary interrogatories. The troops of the King, the military of the Nation, have not this right. As it is, these who guard the *Bastille*, it was necessary to join with them one who was invested with it, in order to proceed to what is there called *Verbal process,* or *Interrogatories,* when they deign to amuse themselves with these formalities. This is the employment of the *Lieutenant of the Police,* and the occasion of the power with which he has been endued.

What is pleasant enough, if anything relative to the *Bastille* can be *so,* what is a farther proof of the consistency of *French* ideas, is, that the robe, which here gives him a title of superiority, excludes every other magistrate from it. The *Chancellor*[7] himself would not be admitted at the *Bastille,* unless indeed he were sent there as a prisoner. When the *Parliament,* (which is sometimes the case, being another consequence of the same judicious principle) accepts *Commissions* in order to give judgement on prisoners lodged in the *Bastille,* the Judges are not allowed to enter the castle; it is at the gate that they hold their session, and that the culprit, or rather the victim, is brought out to them: witness M. *de Lally*[8], *etc.* So that these superior Magistrates, so proud, and so despotic, have not even the right to inspect those places where a subaltern exercises an unbounded authority.

What finally reconciles every kind of contradiction, and surpasses all idea, is, that the acts passed by this Magistrate, expressly called in, expressly instituted, to give them an appearance of *legality,* are formally renounced and proscribed by the Tribunals of which he continues to be a member; and that as often as they are presented to them. They condemn, as illegal and tyrannical, in the *King's* name, on his behalf, and in words they make him speak, those very proceedings which have been carried on in the *King's* name, on his behalf, and in words he is made to speak, by one of their fraternity at the *Bastille;* and even the same man sitting at the *Chatelet*[9] as *Lieutenant of Police,* in the *Parliament* as *Master of Requests,* shall reject with horror, and declare criminal, on the morrow, the very pieces which, in quality of *King's Commissary*[10], he shall have extorted at the *Fauxbourg St. Antoine*[BST], at *Vincennes,* &c. and authenticated with his own signature, the day before.

These absurdities render the *French* Legislation ridiculous in the eyes of foreigners; but unhappily they render it much. more oppressive to the natives.

(5) Page 5. *With the external badge of an honourable service.]* All the officers of the *Etat Major* at the *Bastille* have the *Cross of St. Louis.* Even those who have never served, as the present *Governor,* or who have served under a title which does not confer a right to it, as the present *Major,* have it by honorary grant, apparently made in order to give them a more respectable exterior.

After all, there is nothing astonishing in this. That order, so long respectable and respected, is now conferred even on *Exempts* of the *Police.* This shameful illustration of the most cowardly service that despotism has ever exacted, is to be imputed to Mr. *de Sartines*[BST2]. If the justification of it be taken up on the ground of the occasional utility of these employ-ments, it would be necessary then to render it common to the ordinary *Jailors,* and to the *Hangmen:* for in short they are also useful men; and certainly, in the eyes of reason are infinitely above their comrades of the *Bastille.* they ought to be much less ignominious in the public opinion.

They are only the ministers of an indispensable severity: they are officers, and necessary officers, of a lawful power:

[BST] The Bastille was situated at the Faubourg St. Antoine.
[BST2] Antoine-Raimond-Jean-Gualbert-Gabriel de Sartines (1729-1801) became Lieutenant General of Police in 1759. Known for his efficacy in arranging the police – notably its formidable network of spies – but also for his justice and humanity. He improved the lighting in Paris, among a number of other public works (including, less happily, the building which bore a clock whose decoration shocked Linguet). He was made a State Councillor in 1767. In 1771, he left his position as head of the police and was replaced by Le Noir, whom Linguet frequently mentions. That same year, he became Minister of the Navy, a post he filled less successfully. A conflict with Necker led to his disgrace on October 14, 1980. *Biographie Universelle*, XXXVIII, 36-38.

they may sometimes execute unjust orders; but they act constantly in obedience to justice and the laws. They are certain that the unfortunate being who is delivered to them, either has had, or will have, the means of defending himself: they are sure, or at least must believe, that all equitable and impartial enquiry has preceded the rigorous decision under which they act. They are authorized, to think that none but the guilty, or at least men justly suspected, have ever been the objects of them.

But an *Exempt* of the *Police*, an officer of the *Bastille*, are sure of exactly the contrary: they know that they are violating the laws, and that their special destination is to violate them: they know that three fourths of the victims given to them to crucify are innocent; that if there had been any well-grounded pretext for juridically loading them with chains, the more concise method, by *Lettre-de-cachet*, would not be adopted: they know, in short, were it not for the bayonets which surrounded them, that their process is ready made in the rituals of the Courts of Justice, as well as in the heart of every citizen; and that an ignominious punishment would be the just reward of their infamous compliance.

They know it! and they give themselves up the willing instruments of these outrages, these *Lettres-de-cachet!* The hungry Exempt counts upon his fingers the number of *Louis-d'ors* with which every new prisoner will give him a pretence for swelling his bills: the Jail-Commandant calculates how many *Crowns* he will bring to his kitchen; and both of them find the capture so much the *better*, as it becomes more lucrative to them.

Surely neither the regular executioner, nor his valets, carry the degradation of avarice, and the forgetfulness of every kind of shame, as well as remorse, to such an extreme degree.

Judging then rationally, and submitting prejudice to reflexion, I ask which of these two men must appear more odious in the eyes of society? Which of the two deserves the greater share of contempt and reproach?

(6) Page 7. *Between the Count de Vergennes and me.*] See my Letter to this Minister, printed in 1777[11]. I have not mentioned this letter, nor the noise it has made, as one of the

causes of my imprisonment, because it would be accusing the Count *de Vergennes* point-blank of an imposture, of an hypocrisy; too directly contrary to the virtue, the frankness, of which he makes profession: but it is very true, however, that after I had had the Confident simplicity to repass the sea *upon his parole,* some of my intelligent friends constantly forewarned me of what has happened to me on the 27th of September, 1780: they were incessantly repeating to me, that sooner or later the Count *de Vergennes* would contrive to reconcile the pleasure of revenge with the glory of having appeared to pardon. Ought the conformity between their predictions and the event to preponderate against the confidence inspired by the VIRTUES of the Count *de Vergennes?*

(7) Page 8. *More noble than even that of my residence.]* To reveal the object of this sacrifice, would be to destroy the merit of it. I might be allowed, perhaps, and, it might interest my pride and my revenge, to revoke my word, as the Ministers of *France* have violated theirs: but I have not the honour of being a Minister. An oath tyrannically and unjustly extorted is never binding; a promise voluntarily made must always bind.

(8) Page 8. *With studied and complicated circumstances of ignominy.]* It was in broad day-light, at high noon, in the most public street, the greatest thoroughfare of *Paris,* that I was arrested, before the eyes of ten thousand people brought together in an instant; I might say convoked. My coachman, my footman, or rather those of the *Sieur Le Quesne*[12], and consequently of the *Police,* did not conceal my name from anybody. The malignity of this affection will be felt by those who consider, that on the most serious, nay, the most urgent occasions, it is always an hour of darkness, and secrecy, that is chosen for those violent proceedings: but the ministry, who were seeking vengeance in this, who knew that there was no advantage to be drawn from it, beside the opprobrium and cruelty with which my imprisonment might be accompanied, were resolved to make me drink off the bitter potion, even to its very dregs.

It must be added, that the *Lieutenant* of the *Police,* to whom, according to my usual circumspection and frankness, I had paid my first visit, every time I went to *Paris,* since 1777, had appointed me to be at his house *on that day,* at nine in the evening. We were to have talked of the LXXIst number of the *Annals,* which was not yet distributed. This was the very day on which he caused me to be arrested at noon, with the disgrace which has been just now seen. And after that, they kept me twenty months in impenetrable secrecy; and they made the consequences of this outrage as mysterious as the outrage itself was notorious! What was the object of this? Is it necessary to ask? The openness of the arrest furnished occasion to say, and the mysteriousness of its consequences to believe, every thing against me.

(9) Page 17. The Chargé-d'affaires of FRANCE.] It is not the Count *d'Adhémar*[13], Minister Plenipotentiary from the Court of *France* at *Brussels,* that is here alluded to. I can suppose that a man of condition, who had never had cause to be dissatisfied with me, would on this occasion have supported the dignity of his character, and felt how ill it would become him to associate with the *Familiars* of the *Police* of PARIS, in order to consummate so unjust, and so odious, a system of plunder.

But he was absent: the affair was in the hands of a man named LA GREZE, who is sometimes his steward, sometimes his secretary, &c. and sometimes, his representative; a man whose equivocal birth is his least defect and whose original occupation could not naturally have led him to figure in the *Diplomatic Corps.*

This strange Minister found in the *Exempt* of the *Police* of *Paris,* and in his deputy, two worthy colleagues. He seconded them with all his might, and so much the more easily, as he had it in his power, at least in the first moments, to cover his treacheries under the guise of kindness and friendly zeal. He had, I confess, surprised my confidence: I had not refused it to a man who seemed to have the honour of possessing that of the Government of my Country. He was with me every day, and all the day.

At the instant of the disaster, he was the counselor preferred by the Person, who, sharing it with me, had the further misfortune of being obliged to labour in taking precautions to diminish it.

It may not be impertinent to insert, on this occasion, an anecdote pleasant enough at this hour, but which was not so then.

A principal object was, to save my papers. Not that any thing criminal could have been found in them: but it was my fortune, and more than my fortune. Besides, they contained many important secrets which did not belong to me: the confidence of many worthy people having followed me in my retreat, notwithstanding my absolute renunciation of the Bar; the repose and honour of several families depended on the preservation of my cabinet. *La Greze* being consulted, thought the best expedient was to throw the most valuable of the papers into the imperial of my carriage, to convey them to a country house which I had at three leagues from *Brussels*, and to bury the whole there in the hay with which the lofts were filled: he assisted in *disguise*, at *midnight*, at the execution of his own project constantly repeating *that he was risking his place, and his fortune to render me this service:* he worked himself: he saw the imperial loaded: he was confident that the carriage would depart at the opening of the gates; and was continually swearing, in a tone easily penetrated, that, as he was the sole confident of this deposit, he would be impenetrable.

The carriage did indeed arrive in the country at seven o'clock in the morning. At eight, the *Exempt* of the *Parisian Police* was in my granary: he unhooked the imperial: he broke the padlock: he found there - what? A quantity of straw!

The extreme plausibility affected by *La Greze* in his oaths had betrayed him: and advantage was taken of the moment when he was gone to supper, or rather to inform the Exempt, to make the exchange.

The story is pleasant; but the perfidy was frightful. The following, is if possible, still more atrocious.

In saving such of my papers as were judged the most important; a sufficient quantity bad been left in the house, to give colour to a denial that there were any others. The Police of *Brussels* had seized on this booty, whilst the *Parisian* Agent was in pursuit of one more valuable. He and his accomplice *La Greze* disconcerted by the precaution I have just related, thought to indemnify themselves by getting possession of what remained at *Brussels*. They found resistance in the laws of the country. They wished for a power from me. *Le Quesne*, being called to their aid, had indeed one to produce; but it was old: it had no relation to the event of the moment, nor to its consequences. The Magistrates of *Brusssels* refused to acknowledge it; and my friends yet more strenuously.

It was absolutely necessary to apply to me for a new one: for the itch of coming at my papers was very pressing; and they flattered themselves that under this title they should bring back, even those that had flipped through the net of *La Greze*. It was demanded of me; I refused it point blank. They conjectured my reason. What did they do?

The Sieur La Greze wrote to the *Lieutenant* of the *Police of Paris*, that the justice of *Brussels* had *seized all my effects;* that one part *was already sold,* and CONFISCATED, by virtue of the *Joyous Entry**; that the rest would soon undergo the same fate; and the only means of saving it was a power from me, werewith to oppose these devouring operations. In that place, where nothing is shown, they showed me this letter; they suffered me to drench myself with the gall which it carried to my soul; and they presented me a notary as a comforter.

It was very necessary to obey, where I thought it would be useless to resist. I wished however to limit the procuration thus wrested from me: they made use of violence to oblige me to sign it *general*.

On my arrival at *Brussels* I found that the letter of the Sieur *La Greze* was false in every particular. Nothing had been confiscated: quite the contrary: his accomplices, and their representatives, had alone been concerned in the pillage. The sight of my procuration at *Brussels* caused deep concern; and, though they were unacquainted with the artifices by which it was obtained, they had fortunately made no concessions in consequence of it, except with regard to the articles the least essential to me; my money, for instance, and those *papers* of which the surrender gave me no uneasiness.

---

* It was not mine into the *Bastille* that he spoke of, as will be easily conceived. The *Joyeuse entrée* is a particular right of the Sovereigns of Brabant.

(10) Page 9. *By an Exempt of the Police of Paris.]* To add to this picture of treacheries and meanness, it is proper to observe, that this *Exempt* is one of those whom, in my short and tempestuous career at the Bar, I had rescued from an ill-grounded but virulent persecution. He was chosen, or rather he had offered himself not to serve me; but because, the obligations he had to me being known, and having himself always assumed the exterior of gratitude, he was more proper than another to surprise the credulity of those, whose intelligence, and attachment to me, were to be dreaded.

(11) Page 9. *By a deputy whom I shall elsewhere name.]* This deputy was no other than the *Sieur Le Quesne*. See the particulars of that inconceivable treachery in the *Avis aux Souscripteurs*, which precedes N°. LXXII of the *Annals*[14].

(12) Page 9. *Of the Under-Minister.]* The *Sieur La Greze* caused near 500 livres to be paid him, by *Le Quesne*, at my expence, *for his good offices*. The latter, bringing this article into account against me, informed me that he had paid it *by superior orders*.

(13) Page 10. *It succeeded.]* It will be recollected perhaps that the object of it was to transmit intelligence to the remotest distance, of what kind, or what length soever the dispatches might be, with a rapidity almost equal to that of the imagination.

The only well-grounded objection which has been made to it, is that this aerial post may be interrupted by *fogs* and *snow*. This, I confess but the *snow* continues only for some hours in the year; the *fogs* only some days, at least on the Continent. A river overflown, a bridge broken down, or the fall of a horse, may equally retard for some moments, the ordinary communications.

I will one day make known my ideas on this subject. The invention will certainly admit of being greatly improved, as I have no doubt it will be. I am persuaded that in time it will become the most useful instrument of commerce, and all correspondence of that kind; as *Electricity* will be the most powerful agent of medicine; and as the *Fire-pump* will be the principle of all mechanic processes which require, or are to communicate, great force.

(14) Page 10. *The common rights of Citizen*] "Provided" ! — I am obliged to insist on this restriction. The freedom had been taken of circulating a report, that I had promised indiscriminately *not to write any more;* that this condition had been the price of my liberty. That is not true. The truth is that, being exhausted by this perpetual struggle, this unequal conflict, where, without any weapons but reason and justice, I had continually to encounter with men armed with power and intrigue, I no longer aspired to any thing but a peaceable obscurity. Yet once more; though I was very far from expecting to see two years imprisonment in the *Bastille* succeeded by an unlimited exile, should have patiently awaited at *Rethel* the issue of this new caprice, I should have tried in good earnest to keep silence, or, at least; to *suffer myself to be forgotten,* if they had not presumed to require of me an equal indifference for my civil, as for my literary existence. It is with much regret, but most assuredly without any remorse, that I have again entered on my painful career.

(15) Page 13. *Without example, even at the* Bastille.] I have suppressed many things, of which the recital would not be so striking at this instant, as they must have seemed grievous to me at the time. The juncture is of same moment, even in affliction: a blow which does not affect a man in health, become insupportable; and may prove mortal, if it falls on a limb already broken. But I cannot forbear to insist on the refusal, persevered in to the last of permitting me to make my will *by the means of a public officer.*

If the motive to it was not the most cruel caprice that any Minister was ever licentious enough to give into, its object was a prevarication yet more base: they meant, then by rendering me incapable of disposing of the remains of my fortune, to favour *Le Quesne,* who had the whole in his possession: they intended, if I had died, to spare him the necessity of accounting to my family for more than just what he should have thought proper; and thus to pay for his treacheries, not only at my expence, but at that of my heirs likewise. Having given me no account; having in his hands all my vouchers, all my effects, without exception; being assured, by his connections with the *Police*, &c. that a will written with my own hand would never go out of my sepulcher without his consent; he must certainly have opposed every notarial act, of which it would be more difficult to controul the dispositions, or obliterate the traces.

From which of these two causes did the refusal of the testament arise? I do not know: perhaps they both conduced; but, supposing only one of them, have I not been justified in saying that the refusal was unexampled even in the history of the crimes of the *Bastille?*

(16) Page 20. *Preparing myself a retreat.]* Perhaps nothing short of this last misfortune could have cured me of my extravagant Patriotism: the caustic was violent; but the cure, however, is radical.

Now, that I can laugh, I have been entertained by a simple reflection, which on this occasion escaped a man who acts an important part in the Ministry. When my retreat to London, and my design of publishing these Memoirs were mentioned to him; *But*, says he, *he means then to shut the gates of France against himself forever!* But have these Gentlemen then some more *Lettres-de-cachet* to dispose of; and would they be very solicitous to honour me with the preference?

(17) Page 22. *And made Vengeance drop her arms.]* It is by chance that I have kept a copy of this answer. I must yield to the inclination of giving here at least the conclusion of it. After having particularized, in an affecting manner, the causes that had extorted that letter from me, I added: "He hopes the King will vouchsafe to consider it as a private affair; an affair quite secret, unknown.... that this letter was to be looked upon only as the result of a first emotion, which the laws no where subject to punishment, and for which humanity itself makes allowances; that, in short, in what light soever it is viewed, it ought not to efface the remembrance of those services, which the respondent has all his lifetime assiduously endeavored to render, to the many individuals whom he has defended and saved in the courts of justice; to the public, whom he has laboured to enlighten by his writings; to

religion, to the laws, to morality, which he has always scrupulously respected: nor of that delicacy which led him to sacrifice, on the first approach of the rupture, an establishment already formed in *England*, in order to be nearer to *France;* nor of the firmness with which he has every where diffused the praises, and espoused the interests of his Prince and his Country, even in the midst of their enemies, as his *Annals* particularly evince; nor of the design which he has always entertained, and announced, of returning to *France,* of settling there, of carrying thither his fortune, and of living subject to the laws of the Sovereign under whom Providence had placed him; a design which was one of the principal objects of the present journey, and but for which he should not have fallen into the misfortune he at present labours under."

"One word more, and he will have done. In thus pointing out the considerations which may extenuate his fault, he does not presume, however, wholly to excuse it: he wishes only to offer to the King's clemency some motives for shortening the punishment, and to the M. *de Duras's* generosity, for soliciting the forgiveness of it."

After this answer, I heard not a word more said of it. I only learnt on my enlargement, that it had been matter of pleasantry for the people in office under the Count *de Vergennes,* Amongst others; the Sieur *Moreau,* one of his favorite secretaries, reading it to his friends, gave himself airs at the conclusion, saying, *Hah! hah! he is now playing the Sycophant.*

O *Louis!* just and beneficent Prince, is it thus then that the mercenary agents of those Ministers who deceive you, add insults to the afflictions of your subjects whom they oppress! Is it thus that they dare burlesque the respectful returns of confidence in, and submission to you! Is it thus that an offense, of which twenty months barbarity has been the fruit, is recognized and examined?

(18) Page 22. *Than the satisfaction of having paid it.]* I was assured, after my enlargement, that pretended copies of this letter were in circulation. I here declare, that there is not

possibly a single copy of it extant. It cannot be imagined that the *Lieutenant of the Police* has given it up to public curiosity. Most certainly the Marshal *de Duras* will no more expose it in future, than he has done already. And the hands by which my papers were withdrawn from the eager researches of his avengers, have had the same discretion. Thus this little secret is one of those on which public malignity will never be satisfied.

(19) Page 24. *Of the very ridiculous nephew of M. de Leyrit.]* To be acquainted with this personage, the reader may consult the 8th and 9th volumes of the *Annals*, particularly the 9th, at the 217th and following pages. Few lawsuits have been more atrocious, and none, even in *France*, has been more unaccountable, in its circumstances and its consequences, than the whole process of *M. de Lally*[BST]. The *Parliament* of *Paris*, after having had the inconsistent meanness to accept a *commssion* to judge him, and the horrid barbarity to punish him, by a sentence of death, for some sallies of passion, excusable perhaps in every point of view, for some extravagancies which the very sentence dared not to denominate a crime, has had at once the meanness and the cruelty clandestinely to thwart a son in his petition to take off the stigma from his father's memory.

The *Parliament* of *Rouen*, appointed to revise a sentence already acknowledged irregular in point of form, already annulled in consequence, and demonstrated to be at least as unjust in its form, did not, indeed, so far prevaricate as to dare to confirm it; but, in order to elude the necessity of

---

[BST] Thomas Arthur, Count de Lally, (1702-1766) was a French general of Irish descent who had had a distinguished career, but was put on trial after surrendering Pondicherry to the English. He spent most of his imprisonment in the Bastille, but was transferred to the Conciergerie the day of his execution (which was a bloody, botched affair). – Trophime Gérard, marquis de Lally-Tollendal, (1751-1830) learned on the day of Lally's execution that he was the general's son. He made it his mission to clear his father's name, and in the process became a major figure in French public life. With Voltaire's help, he had an initial success, only to see the case sent on to other venues, including the Parlements of Rouen and then (as Linguet writes here) Dijon. *Biographie Universelle*, XXII, 639-656.

deciding between justice, and a body of men of their own order, they chose rather to violate one of the most solemn regulations in the *French* practice, and to admit an *interposition* equally strange in its circumstances and absurd in itself, as insupportable in jurisprudence: whence result new contests, new questions, a new reference to another Parliament, that of *Dijon*, where M. *de Lally* will have to combat the same prejudices, the same deference for the spirit of party, and the same animosities.

It cannot be too often repeated, that, the rest of the universe affords no parallel instances, they are not admitted, they cannot be admitted, any where but in *France*.

Sic vivitur illic.[15]

But they have also there the *Comic Opera*, the *Grand Opera*, the *Boulevards*, the *Elysian Fields*, the *Mercury*, &c. &c. &c.[16]

(20) Page 25. *Whilst I wrote from England, I was exposed to none of these broils.]* This remark is no less true than singular; and it alludes to an anecdote yet more extraordinary, if possible, than all that has preceded, but which I suppress for two reasons: 1° Through respect to an august name, which must other wise be brought forward; 2° Because it is more curious, more poignant, than useful. The only thing it would prove, is the superiority which the influence of an atmosphere purified by Liberty, such as that of *Great Britain*, gives even to individuals, over the foulness of Despotism, which corrupts and enervates almost equally its agents, and its victims. Now does this want demonstration.

(21) Page 30. *So tedious an atonement.]* I am exceedingly concerned to keep the Marshal de *Duras* so long on a stage where he does not cut a very honourable figure, but once more it is not my fault. To reduce me to eternal silence, he had only to have been generous for a single moment.

MEMOIRS

OF

THE BASTILLE

PART II.

SECTION III.

Of the Regimen of the Bastille.

I SHALL not at present touch on that tender question, of which the discussion would be more difficult than the solution could be useful; I shall not examine whether State-Prisons be necessary appendages to a Government; whether every Administration require these fastnesses, removed without the pale, and withdrawn from the inspection of the Laws; whether this spring, for the most part violent, and always dangerous, may be considered as an indispensable requisite of machines which for their preservation sometimes stand in need of an extraordinary impulse; whether, in fine, what is in France known by the strange appellation of a *Letter-de-cachet*, be an evil peculiar to that kingdom, like the plague in Egypt, the smallpox in Arabia, and those inundations of liquid fire in the countries infested by burning mountains? This problem is best resolved by facts; and although such solution may not be admitted by humane philosophy, it is nevertheless adopted by universal policy.

We are unacquainted with a nation among whom this

resource, or else some equivalent, has not been an engine in the bands of power. In the purest area of her liberty, Rome had her Dictators. The orders of this supreme magistrate bore an authority not inferior to that of a *Lettre-de-cachet*, since he disposed without appeal, and without responsibility, not only of the Liberty, but even of the lives of the citizens.

In Sparta we may observe how State-policy extended still farther the bounds of despotism The Kings themselves, that is to say, the Chiefs of the nation, bowed before it. The EPHORI[1] had power to commit them to prison ; and though their warrant varied somewhat from a *Lettre-de-cachet*, yet, in its principle, it may be considered as essentially the same.

Nay, in that part of the world where the Government is most closely watched and restrained, where the privileges of individuals are most effectually secured from the incroachments of arbitrary power.; in London itself, we behold a TOWER destined for the reception of State-Criminals. The Parliament, that guardian of private, no less than of public freedom, not only sees without terror, a citadel that seems to threaten destruction to both, but even goes so far sometimes to use it; and in so doing they are not thought to violate, nor yet to hazard the liberty of the People. *(Note* 1.)

But a similar institution may appear to be far more excusable in France; where, the characters of men being more impetuous, the pretensions of different powers continually jarring with each other less circumscribed, and the regal authority neither limited nor ascertained, we may easily conceive, that on some occasions, it will be necessary to have a check, or kind of scare-crow to defend the prerogative of the Crown, if not of the Kingdom. But I once more observe, that this is a point which I do not pretend to examine: I am not to confider the legality of the institution, but the regimen of the BASTILLE ; I mean, the exercise of its authority. Now its regimen is dreadful; it resembles nothing practised heretofore, or at this moment practiced, in the known world. (2)

If in one of those relations, which the ebullitions of imaginary travelers have multiplied of late years[2], we should read, that in an island of the southern hemisphere, which nature seems to have concealed from the rest of the-globe, there exists a people, gay, mild, and frivolous, not only in their manners, but also in their most essential qualities with a Government far from sanguinary; where the most serious affairs ever assume an air of pleasantry; and in whose capital notwithstanding, is kept with infinite care, an abyss, into which every citizen, without exception, is each moment liable to be hurled, and into which some are actually precipitated every day, in consequence of orders inevitable, as they are inexplicable; for which it is often impossible to divine the motive or the pretext:

That the unfortunate wretch thus vanished, finds himself detached from all the *rest* of mankind; farther removed from his relations, from his friends, and, what is worse than all, from justice, than if he had been transferred into another planet; that his cries and supplications are stifled in their passage, or at least, that only one channel is allowed for their issue, and that precisely the one most interested in suppressing them; a motive, that must be prevalent, in proportion as the oppression is palpable and enormous:

That he is abandoned, at least for a considerable length of time; without books, without paper, to the torturing suspense of being entirely ignorant of what passes in the world, of the fate of his family, his fortune, his honour; of what he has been, and of what he is to be accused; torments which a perpetual solitude, undiverted by any kind of avocation, renders more intolerable:

That he has no other security for his life but the tenderness of his keepers, who, notwithstanding the mark of honour attached to their habit, being capable of such meanness as to become for hire the base satellites of arbitrary power, would doubtless feel but little repugnance in undertaking an office still more base and barbarous, if it was required of them on the same terms: that he has therefore grounds to be apprehensive of poison in every dish that is served up to him: that every time his door is opened the melancholy clang of the bolts and bars with which it is loaded, may seem to announce his death-warrant, or to notify the arrival of the mutes destined to perform the fatal office; whilst he cannot derive the least motive to tranquility either from the consciousness of his innocence, or from the equity of the Sovereign; since the first attack on the former, may be followed by a second; since they have the same power over his life, as they exercise over his Liberty; since the same persons, who a thousand times a day lend their hands to his execution in a moral sense, by virtue of a *Lettre-de-cachet*, could not be supposed to refuse their assistance to accomplish the same purpose in a literal sense, when once commissioned by the same authority; and lastly, since in a place where all is mystery and sorrow, there is no enormity so atrocious, but may with as much ease be concealed as committed.

That, if he preserves his health, it is but an additional grievance, sensibility being then more exquisite, and privation more painful; that if it gives way, as is generally the case, to the miseries of his situation, he is allowed neither relief nor comfort; but must remain in that helpless and wretched condition; perpetually agonized by reflecting on the impossibility of an escape, on the misfortune that may happen to his family, the oblivion to which his name is in danger of being consigned; by considering, that his ashes will be deprived of the last sad tribute of tenderness and affection; that his end will perhaps be unknown; and that his mistaken wife and children may be offering up vows and making efforts for his deliverance, long after the sepulchre, in which he was buried alive will contain no remains of him but his bones!

Should we find such a picture in the voyages of Cooke, or Anson, what sort of impression would it make upon our minds[3]? Might we not take the author for an *impostor;* or in felicitating ourselves on being natives of a country exempt from such a wretched servitude, should We not conceive a degree of contempt, mingled with horror, for a Government so barbarous, and a People so debased?

But, alas! it is the picture of no other than the BASTILLE, and that far from overcharged! How weakly does it represent those tortures and lengthened convulsions of the mind; those perpetual agonies that eternize the pains of death, without affording it repose; in short, all the torments which the jailors of the Bastille can inflict, and which no stretch of human art can exhibit!

Secrecy of imprisonment

The first article of their code is the impenetrable mystery with which all their operations are inveloped; a mystery that goes so far, as not only to leave people in doubt with regard to the place of residence, but even with regard to the life, of the unfortunate person who has flipped into their hands; a mystery that is not confined to the interdiction of all communication, whence he might derive either comfort or amusement, but is carried to such extent, as to prevent it from being known with certainty where he is, or even whether he is still in existence[BST].

A prisoner, whom an officer of the Bastille sees every day, will, when spoken of in the world, be denied with consummate effrontery ever to have been seen or known by him. When some of my faithful friends solicited of the Minister who presides over these dungeons, permission to visit me, he asked, as it were with astonishment, how they could suppose me to be in the Bastille? The Governor has often sworn to several of them, on his word and honour as a Gentleman, that I was no longer confined there, and that I had not been detained there above eight days; for the public notoriety of my apprehension, and the care they had taken to have it executed by broad day-light and in the open street,

---

[BST] This was not uniformly true. Some prisoners were even allowed visits, though a visitor needed a letter from the Lieutenant of Police, specifying the number and duration of their visits. Bastille personnel stood between the visitor and the prisoner, unless special permission had been granted (it rarely was) for a private visit. *Mémoires de Linguet*, 197. Around the start of the eighteenth century, one official complained about having to fetch prisoners from their room "crossing all the courtyards", deliver them to the governor's room, then wait outside, "usually up until eight hours" to return the prisoner. Bournon, 268.

would not permit him to maintain, as without doubt he otherwise would have done, that, I had never entered the walls of the prison.

Thus a porter will often declare a falsehood at his master's gate, in obedience to his orders: but this is merely to prevent importunate visits; his falsehoods have an end, either of utility or convenience; he neither maintains them with an affected air of sincerity, nor with oaths: and, notwithstanding, his employ is thought a vile one. What then must be that of a Minister, of a Governor of the Bastille, who deceives but to torment, and whose falsehoods are productive of nothing but affliction?

I should be glad to be informed, what can be the design of all this affectation of mystery, in leaving the public at large, friends, relations, doubtful of the very being of a man whom they have ravished from them? it cannot be to facilitate the means of convicting him, and to render his punishment the more certain: for, first, this clandestine custody can be of no avail to those who are employed against him elsewhere, either to carry on the prosecution, or to execute the sentence pronounced upon him: secondly, My example proves, that the Bastille often contains prisoners whom they not only never intend to prosecute, but whom they even have not wherewithal to arraign; and it is precisely these, whom they are most assiduous to cover with a veil of darkness, I repeat it once more, what can the design be?

The express institution of this prison being to distract the mind, and to render life itself miserable, (as one of my tormentors once ingenuously acknowledged, a man, who, though honoured with the order of St. Louis[4], had not virtue enough to shudder at the idea of so horrid a function;) I conceive that this dreary solitude, this absolute ignorance in which they keep a prisoner with respect to what has been done, is actually doing, or is about to be done, either for or against him, are means admirably adapted to the end proposed. Nothing can be contrived or imagined more effectual to lead a man through each gradation of despair;

particularly, if he has the misfortune to be endowed with one of those lofty and active souls, which are apt to be shocked with a virtuous indignation at injustice, to which employment is a want, and suspence a punishment. But why make partakers of his torments, friends and relations, whom they pretend not to associate in his affliction?

When a process is established, there is at least this alleviation that the nature and extent of the accusation is known, the progress of the proceeding, regular and open[5]; the victim is not lost to view, till his sacrifice or his triumph. Disquiet has its bounds and grief its consolation.

But here, whilst the wretch removed from every eye accuses his family and friends of neglecting him, they are trembling lest their remembrance of him should be imputed to them as a crime; his captivity depending on caprice, and his chains being liable to be knocked off every moment, or to be perpetuated without end, each day is to those who long to see him, as it is to the unfortunate man himself, a complete period, in which they exhaust all the anguish of suspence, all the horrors of privation: in the morning their tears flow on the recollection of his suferings, and in the evening on the anticipation of what he is yet to suffer: while it is impossible for them to conceive when they will terminate: or, if the imagination should attempt to fix their bounds, it is but a preparation of renovated misery.

The Tyrant, who first founded this prison, had his view in so horrid an institution; which was to get rid, with all possible privacy, of such persons as the executioners themselves would refuse to assassinate[BST]. When he had once proscribed

---

[BST] The Bastille was not built by the 'Tyrant' referred to - Louis XI (1423-1483) -, but by Charles V, in 1370, at the suggestion of the provost of Paris, Hughes Aubriot – who briefly became the first prisoner there, though its original intent was defensive. Gourdon, 4. Sinister stories are often told about Louis XI which may be why Linguet seems to credit him here with founding the castle. This is a typical account: "The cruel and moody character of Louis XI prompted him to invent a ghastly cell for prisoners of distinction held in the Bastille. He treated them like wild animals by having them locked in iron cages only a foot higher than a

an innocent person, for the innocent only are proscribed, wilst the guilty are judged, he wished to have the epoch of his death unknown, that he might fix it precisely at the very moment most agreeable to his interest or his vengeance.

But Lewis XVI is not Lewis XI, the one is as humane, as the other was barbarous; the one respects as much justice and the laws, recommends and enjoins as urgently the observation fo them, as the other took delight in having them trampled on, and giving himself the example of the violation. Whence then does it arrive, that the humanity of Lewis XVI connives at the continuance of an institution invented by the tyranny of Lewis XI? How comes it that under a Prince to whom law is sacred, and the blood of mankind precious, his subjects are liable to the same catastrophe as they were under a Sovereign to whom an execution was a favorite amusement, who called the executioner his *Cousin*[6], and never went abroad but under the escort of a Satellite, another of his cousins, but more savage and sanguinary than all the executioners together?

Further, if it was the enormity of the crime, or the rank of the delinquent, that should require this strange and perilous concealment; if this funeral veil was thrown only over those whom the magnitude of their offences had devoted to immediate punishment, or over those who, given to intrigue and cabal, might be formidable from their birth, their riches or their connexions; there would be some excuse, or at least some pretext for it.

But the Bastille, like death, brings to an equality all whom it swallows up: the sacrilegious villain, who has plotted the destruction of his Country; the undaunted Patriot, guilty of no other crime but that of maintaining her rights with too much ardour; the Wretch, who has betrayed for gold the

---

man's head. The inmate was loaded with shackles and a heavy chain at the end which he dragged a ball. The first condemned to this horrible stay was a bishop of Verdun, who spent fourteen years there. Prisoners of war whose escape Louis XI feared were also detained in these awful dwellings. The huge chains which they dragged around were called the 'king's little girls'." Frégier, I, 476

secrets of the cabinet, and he who has dared to speak truths to Ministers, useful to the State, but repugnant to their interest: as well he who is confined lest he should become a dishonour to his family, as he who is only obnoxious on account of his talents, are all overwhelmed alike in uniform darkness[BST].

Ignorance of the outside world

And, let it be considered well; this darkness is double: it prevents them from seeing, no less than from being seen; it not only deprives the prisoner of the knowledge of every thing that personally interests him, of the power of inspecting the state of his private affairs of preventing either by definitive or provisional arrangements his own ruin, and sometimes that of his correspondents; and, above all, that of informing his friends, and confuting his enemies; in short, of every kind of useful occupation; but it also covers from his sight the view of public affairs, and every thing else that might have a tendency to amuse or divert his solitude. Become an outcast from society he is not permitted even to know what is going forward in the world. There may perhaps be in these dungeons, a man, who is daily solliciting with his prayers Lewis XV and the Duke *de la Vrillière*[7]; he thinks them still the living forgers of his chains: he is incessantly on his

---

[BST] Berville and Barrière say "The Bastille has held wily crooks, clever schemers, audacious adventurers and great scoundrels." *Mémoires de la Bastille*, 52n. More scientifically, Lüsebrink and Reichardt write "Concerning the Bastille, the prison statistics contradict the impression of overflowing dungeons and increasing despotic arbitrariness created by the scandal reports of everyone from Renneville to Latude. Between the reign of Louis XIV and that of Louis XVI, the number of captives was halved, while the average period of confinement dropped from three years to between one and two months. So the approximately fifty cells of the Bastille were hardly filled in the first half of the eighteenth century; toward the end of the ancien régime most of them were empty. Apart from confinements for religious reasons... arrests were usually based on valid laws..." These authors also offer figures for some of the causes of imprisonment from 1661 to 1789, noting largely religion (Protestants, Jansenists and Convulsionnaires) and producing and distributing banned works, and from 1749-1789, production and distribution of banned books, religious reasons, criticism of the king, his family, court, or government and fraud, immorality or madness. Lüsebrink, 28-29.

knees before the images of those two persons, of whom nothing remains at present but the memory; and the officers of the prison, witnesses of his error, are so stupidly reserved, or so cruelly scrupulous, as not to acquaint him with it[BST].

From this total ignorance of what is, and what is not, there results an infinity of effects calamitous to the deceived and unfortunate prisoner. For example, if he has been sacrificed to the personal vengeance of a man in power, he has not the consolation of beholding the fall of a colossus, whose elevation has be en fatal to him. Neither can he take the advantage of it, since it is a circumstance which he is entirely uninformed of: and, if he has not very zealous friends; if his family is timid or obscure, indifferent or disaffected to him; the oppression still subsists, although the oppressor is no more. The successor turns his thoughts rather to the exertion of the same authority, than to remove the evils it has occasioned. The prisoner continues immured in the Bastille, not because it is intended that he should remain there; but because he is there, because he is forgotten; because interest is not made at the proper offices; and because nothing equals the difficulty of getting out of that murderous pit, except the facility of falling into it.

I can produce an example, besides my own, and that without calling anyone into question. Whilst I was in the Bastille there was a native of Geneva, by name *Pelisseri*[BST2], confined there. His sole crime was, having made some remarks on Mr. Necker's operations in the finance department. When I was by a very extraordinary accident informed of it, he had already been three years in the prison. Probably he is there still; and knows neither of the ruin of his Country, nor that of the Minister, whom he justly accuses of

---

[BST] After a madman attacked Louis XV, the Lieutenant of Police (Berryer) wrote the Governor: "Instruct the officers of the Bastille to forbid all those who receive permission to speak to the prisoners to talk, in any manner whatsoever, of this horrible event *on pain of immediately being kept as a prisoner in the castle.*". When the Bastille was freed, one prisoner asked if Louis XV (dead since 1774) was still alive. *Mémoires de Linguet*, 54n, 55n.
[BST2] See Appendix D. for more about this Genevan prisoner.

his own. There too perhaps he will continue, till chance, or possibly the mention I now make of him, may recall his memory to the minds of those moveable masters, who can over-rule the immobility of the Bastille: perhaps they will at length be sensible how shocking it is to humanity and justice, that the name of the STATE should give a sanction to perpetuate the personal vengeance of a temporary Minister; that a stranger, an honest man, should be punished, for having been so enlightened, as to foresee what the Government should before have been well apprised of. For after all, what remains of the operations of Mr. Necker? If Mr. *Pelisseri* has been culpable in censuring them, what must those be who have destroyed them? (3)

Can one *reflect* without shuddering, that the horrors I am now tracing have been the reward of an indiscretion, which a few months later would have been an action, not only of prudence, but of necessity? The panegyrist of Mr. Necker would, doubtless, in the present state of affairs, soon be made a fellow-captive with his accuser: thus, whilst a despotism unrestrained by shame, multiplies at its discretion the victims of these dangerous and inconclusive speculations, their cries and supplications die away in the inaccessible avenues of the prison.

Prisoners incommunicado

Again, let it be observed, that, as nothing can get admission, so nothing can find its way out of it[BST]: the very attempts which a prisoner may hazard, to procure, by means of his friends or patrons, either a pardon or a trial are intercepted and smothered: should he be so indiscreet as to hint the quarter from which he may look for succour, the

---

[BST] This is an exaggeration, though not completely untrue. But when Linguet refused to eat because he was afraid of being poisoned (see below), it was discussed in the press soon after his arrest. A bit later, on October 17, 1780, Bachaumont wrote: "It is known that Me. Linguet is still in the Bastille, because though his letters are not exactly received, fragments concerning the articles he has requested from Monsieur Le Quesne for his use and needs are; apparently he is even very indiscreet in what he writes in this prison, so that only extracts are released and the originals do not arrive." Bachaumont, Tome XVI, 17, 26.

blood-hounds of the Police hasten to block up the passage, and to obstruct the efforts that might be undertaken in his favour. They never leave it in his power to solicit those who are in a capacity to make interest for him, until he has exhausted, to the last drop, the bitter draught which despotism and hatred have prepared for him.

His letters, when he is allowed the means of writing, pass open to the *Police*, or are there broke open. The doleful lamentations of the captives afford no small amusement to the persons appointed to inspect them: they divert themselves for a short time with the various notes of the different birds they have in their cage[BST], and then tie up carefully in a bundle together the several epistolary productions of the day; not to be applied to any use, but either to deposit them in some hidden magazines, or to burn them: and neither the persons who wrote them, nor those to whom they are addressed ever see them or hear of them afterwards[BST2].

In the commencement of my captivity I resolved on imploring the favour of the Princes of the Blood Royal. Having been beforehand informed, that Monsieur and the Count of d'Artois[8] honoured me with their esteem, I flattered myself that they would extend their bounty to me in my misfortunes. I consequently wrote to them, and sealed up the letters. Some time after, I was informed by the Lieutenant of the Police, that he had read my letters, but had not delivered them; that he had not the authority to do so. On which I observed that, as he knew the substance, he might make those noble Princes, from who they were withheld,

---

[BST] It seems unlikely that, if this were so, Linguet would have known it. The official remarks preserved in the Archives are never mocking. Individual turn-keys or other officials could of course be unpleasant, as could certain governors, but no official attitude of this sort can be documented.

[BST2] This was essentially true, with exceptions. One unsent letter found in the archives ended with this poignant postscript: "If for my peace of mind, my lord would allow me, in the name of the Holy Trinity, to have news of my dear wife, just her name on a card, to let me know she is still alive: this would be the greatest consolation I could receive..." *Mémoires de Linguet*, 58n.

acquainted with it. To this he replied, that he had not access to men of their high rank. So a person not deemed worthy of approaching these great men, was allowed the liberty of opening their letters, of suppressing them, of rendering their good intentions and those of the King futile; in fine, of raising around me ramparts more insurmountable than all the magic castles, with which imagination has filled the regions of romance!

Arrival at the Bastille

Let us now enter into the inside of these ramparts: let us now examine how those three-headed monsters, who guard them, as in the accomplishment of their abominable office, to render life an insupportable burthen.

The prelude to their operations, when a fresh victim is brought to them, is the *Search*[BST]. Their mode of taking possession of a prisoner's person, and their manner of shewing him the infernal property in which he will be held, is first to strip him of all his own. He is no less astonished, than alarmed to find himself delivered up to the searching and groping of four men, whose appearance is enough to belie their functions, and yet does but add to their infamy; of four men decorated with a uniform, which must give one cause to expect decency of conduct, with insignia, I repeat once more, which one would suppose to denote an *honourable* service.

They take away his money, least it should afford the means of corruption amongst them; his jewels, on the very same consideration; his papers, lest they should furnish him with a resource against the weariness and vexation to which he is doomed; his knives, scissors, &c. least he should cut his own throat, say they, or assassinate his jailors: for they explain to him coolly the motives for all their depredations. After this

---

[BST] With minor variations, this is the same process described by others. The official rules stated "When a prisoner arrives and he is in the castle chamber, he is made to empty his pockets on the table. He is made to turn them inside out all the way to the gussets of his breeches: if he is a good-for-nothing who justly inspires caution, the turn-key searches him to see that he has hidden nothing; after which his entry is processed and all his papers noted, etc., etc." *La Bastille dévoilée*, II, 34, cited in *Mémoires de Linguet*, 60n.

ceremony, which is long, and often interrupted by pleasantries and remarks on every article in the inventory, they drag him to the cell destined for his reception.

Cells

These cells are all contained in towers of which the walls are at least twelve, and at the bottom thirty or forty feet thick. Each has a vent-hole made in the wall; but crossed by three grates of iron, one within, another in the middle, and a third on the outside. The bars cross each other, and are an inch in thickness; and by a refinement of invention in the persons who contrived them, the solid part of each of these meshes answers exactly to the vacuity in another; so that a passage is left to the sight, of scarcely two inches, though the intervals are near four inches square[BST].

Formerly each of these caves had three or four openings, small indeed, and ornamented with the same gratings. But this multiplicity of holes was soon found to promote the circulation of their air; they prevented humidity, infection, &c. A humane Governor therefore had them stopped up; and at present there remains but one, which on very fine days just admits light enough into the cell to make "darkness visible".

So in winter these dungeons are perfect ice-houses, because they are lofty enough for the frost to penetrate; in summer they are moist suffocating stoves, the walls being too thick for the heat to dry them[BST].

[BST] No one else consulted here seems to have noticed this placement of the bars. But the general description matches other accounts, though some windows seemed to have had better views. Several sources confirm that the windows were increasingly blocked or sealed off completely over time, though by several governors, not just one. Renneville mentions one case where a grate was added inside after a prisoner had signaled from his window and another where a new governor completely sealed several windows, in part because water had been coming in. Savine, 85, 117, 178. After an attempted escape in 1779, De Launay had double sets of bars put on all the windows. Arnould, VI, 146, 159. As the Bastille was being torn down, cannonballs were found blocking some windows as well. *Mémoires de la Bastille*, 245.

[BST] The climate in the rooms varied both over time and between rooms. The *calottes* – the dome-shaped rooms at the top of each tower – were said to be freezing in winter and stifling in summer. *Mémoires de Linguet*, 245.

Several of the cells, and mine was of the number, are situated upon the ditch into which the common sewer of the *Rue St Antoine* empties itself[BST2]; so that whenever it is cleared out, or in summer after a few day continuance of the hot weather, or after an inundation, which is frequent enough both spring and autumn in ditches sunk below the level of the river, there exhales a most infectious, pestilential vapour: and when it has once entered those pidgeon-holes they call rooms, it is a considerable time before they are cleared of it.

Such is the atmosphere a prisoner breathes; there in order to prevent a total suffocation, is he obliged to pass his days, and often his nights, stuck up against the interior grate, which keeps him from approaching, as described above, too close to the hole cut in the form of a window; the only orifice through which he can draw his scanty portion of air and of light. His efforts to suck a little fresh air through this narrow tube serve often but, to encrease around him the fetid *odour*, with which he is on the point of being suffocated.

Inadequate heat

But woe to the unfortunate wretch, who in winter cannot procure money to pay for the firing, which they distribute in the *King's name*[BST]! Formerly a proper quantity was supplied

---

Boucquoy found the summer weather there fine, perhaps because less windows were blocked in his time? Du Noyer, 146. The subterranean cachots – which were generally used as punishments – were predictably cold in winter. During one stay, Renneville said the water in his pitcher froze. Savine, 156.

[BST2] The ditch (moat) was often dry, but could fill when the river overflowed. Bernaville blocked the windows on the ground floor in part because prisoners found themselves standing in water. Savine, 178. When Bucquoy escaped, it seemed to be dry. Du Noyer, 166-168. Latude intentionally chose a night when the ditch was full: "We set [our escape attempt] for Wednesday, February 25, 1755, the night before Fat Thursday. Then, the river was overflowing, there were four feet of water in the ditch of the Bastille and in that of the St. Antoine Gate." Masers de Latude, 63.

[BST] Like food, heat and firewood seemed to have varied greatly depending on a prisoner's status. Renneville quotes one particularly ill-treated prisoner as saying: "He swore to us he hadn't seen fire for two years, which surprised me enormously, I not knowing that I would be seven

for the consumption of each prisoner; without equivalent, and without measure. They were not used to cavil with men in every other respect deprived of all, and subjected to so cruel a privation of exercise, on the quantity of fire requisite to rarefy their blood coaguelated by inaction, and to volatise the vapours condensed upon their walls. It was the will of the Sovereign, that they should enjoy the benefit of this solace, or this refreshment, unrestrained as to the expence.

The intention, without doubt, is still the same: yet is the custom altered. The present Governor has limited the proportion for each prisoner to six billets of wood, *great or small.* It is well known, that in Paris the logs for chamber use are but half the market size, being sawed through the middle: they are no more than eighteen inches in length. The econimical purveyor is careful to pick out in the timber-merchants' yards the very smallest he can find, and, what is as incredible as it is true, the very worst. He chuses in preference those at the bottom of the piles, which are exhausted by time and moisture of all their salts, and for that reason thrown aside to be sold at an inferior price to the brewers, bakers, and such other trades as require a fire rather clear than substantial. Six of those logs, or rather sticks, make the allowance of four and twenty hours for an inhabitant of the Bastille.

It may be asked, what they do when this allowance is exhausted? They do as the honourable Governor advises them; they put up with their sufferings. (4)

---

years without coming near any fire but that of a candle." Savine, 55, 87-88. Madame de Staal, a well-treated prisoner overall, complains only that she had passed the winter in an apartment without a tapestry (for insulation). Staal, 439. Dumouriez does say at one point that his room was 'glacial' but on the next page he describes using a firebrand from his fire in a fight with a guard. II, 274-275. He was more intent on firewood as an indicator of the number of prisoners: "It was winter, and every Saturday they brought, to the foot of each tower, as many piles of wood as there were occupied rooms. By observations in this regard, he calculated how many companions of misfortune there were in each tower....there were never in his time more than nineteen, and during several days there were only seven." II, 291.

Furniture and decoration

The articles of furniture are worthy of the light by which they are exhibited, and the apartments they serve to decorate. I must first observe, that the Governor contracts with the Ministry to supply them; and this is one of the trifling perquisites attached to his immense revenue, which I shall take notice of presently. He may frame excuses for himself, with regard to the inconveniences of the prison, because he cannot change the situation of places; he may palliate the niggardly distribution of wood; under the pretext of saving the King's money; but on the head of furniture, which is entirely his own affair, and for which he is paid, he can have neither excuse nor palliation: his parsimony in this particular is at the same time both cruel and dishonest!

Two mattrasses half eaten by the worms, a matted elbow chair, the bottom of which was kept together by pack-thread, a tottering table, a water pitcher, two pots of Dutch ware, one of which served to drink out of, and two flagstones to support the fire, composed the inventory of mine[BST]. I was indebted only to the commiseration of the turnkey, after several months confinement, for a pair of tongs and a fire-shovel. I could not possibly procure dog-irons; and whether it may be considered as the effect of policy, or want of feeling, what the Governor does not think proper to furnish, he will not suffer the prisoner to provide at his own expence. It was eight months ere I could gain permission to purchase a tea-pot; twelve before I could procure a chair tolerably steady and convenient; and fifteen ere I was allowed to replace, by a vessel of common ware, the clumsy and disgusting pewter machine they had assigned me.

The sole article I was allowed to *purchase* in the beginning

---

[BST] The furniture was rarely praised. Dumouriez: "An old bed of very bad and very dirty serge, a close-stool, a wooden table, a straw chair and a pitcher were all its furnishings." (II, 28). The *Bastille devoilée* lists the following as standard: "A bed of green serge with curtains of the same; a straw mat and a mattress; a table or two, two pitchers, a candleholder and a tin goblet; two or three chairs, a fork, a spoon and everything needed to light a fire; by special favor, weak little tongs and two large stones for an andiron." (*La Bastille devoilée*, cited in Coeuret, 54-55).

of my imprisonment, was a new blanket; and the manner by which I obtained this privilege was as follows.

It is well known that in the month of September the moths which prey upon woolen stuffs are transformed into butterflies. On the opening of the cave into which I was introduced, there arose from the bed, I will not say a number, or a cloud, but a large thick column, of these insects, which instantly overspread the whole chamber. The sight caused me to start back with horror; when I was consoled by one of my conductors with the assurance, *that before I had lain there two nights, there would not be one left*.

In the evening the Lieutenant of the Police came according to custom, to bid me welcome; when I expressed *such* a violent dislike to a flock-bed so full of incumbents, that they were graciously pleased to *permit* me to put on a new covering, and to have the mattrass beaten, all at *my own expence*. As feather-beds are entirely prohibited in the Bastille, no doubt, less because they are considered as too great a luxury for persons to whom the Ministry wishes to give a lesson of mortification, I was very desirous that every three months my miserable mattrass should be suffered to undergo the same kind of renovation. Yet the proprietary Governor opposed it with all his might not withstanding it would have cost him nothing, "for", said he, "we must not use them to too much indulgence."

Madame de Staal informs us that she got her room lined with tapestry. Whether she owed this condescension to her quality as the favourite of a great Princess, or to the manners of the age, which retained even in the Bastille some tincture of humanity, as may be inferred from other circumstances in her relation, I shall not take upon me to determine. Thus much is certain; that all these indulgences are now considered as abuses, which were to be retrenched by the fierce regularity of modern times. My urgent applications to obtain at my own expense either some cloth to absorb the moisture of the walls, or paper, whence I might have derived the same benefit, with the further amusement of pasting it on myself, were made and repeated to no effect.

In my chamber the walls had a most dismal appearance. One of my predecessors, whether a painter by profession, or one who cultivated the art for his amusement, got *leave* to daub over the apartment, after a manner; and he at any rate had the satisfaction not to be totally excluded from every *thing* to *employ* his hands, or occupy his attention. The chamber is an octagon, with four large and four small sides: they are all lined with pictures very suitable to the place; namely, the representation of our *Saviour's* sufferings.

But whether through *choice*, or because they would allow him but the one colour adapted to the subject and the apartment, he had done them all in oker; whence their gloomy uniformity may be easily imagined. After the flight of the butterflies, when I cast my eyes on those pannels, which the obscurity of the chamber rendered still more dismal, and could discern nothing but figures of grief, punishment and execution, without distinguishing the particular subject, what we have heard of the *Oubliettes*[*], what we know of the *Sambenitos*[†] instantly recurred to my imagination: and I firmly believed that those figures were so many emblems of the lot

---

[*] The Count *de Boulainvilliers* says, in one of his letters, that the Bastille was destined for prisoners, whose destruction was resolved on; either by apparent forms of justice, or by the punishment of the *Oubliettes;* a method much practiced by *Tristan l'Hermite,* Provost of the Hotel, and companion of Lewis XI, whom the author alludes to above,: when speaking of Lewis' satellite ——This man, of execrable memory, was himself judge, witness, and executioner. He caused the victims, which were delivered to him by Lewis, to be placed on a trap-door, through which they fell on wheels armed with points and cutting edges: others were drowned with a stone about their necks, or stifled in dungeons. This tyrant put to death more than four thousand people in this manner.

There is also in the castle of *Ruel,* which was Cardinal Richelieu's country seat, and at present belongs to the Duke of d'Aiguillon, a closet that still preserves the name of *Cabinet des Oubliettes*. This Minister caused the persons whom he had doomed to destruction to enter it; which they had scarcely done, when a trap-door in the floor opened under their feet, and they instantly fell into a profound abyss. *vide* HOWARD ON PRISONS.

[†] The sack, hood, or bonnet, put upon the victims destined to death by the Inquisition. It was of a saffron colour, with two crosses on it, and the representation of the devil, and the flames of hell.

which awaited me, and that they had put me in this dungeon to prepare me for it. I commended myself to the mercy of the Almighty. Souls endued with sensibility judge of the horrors of the moment.

Isolation of prisoners

Thus provided as to furniture and lodging, if the captives were but allowed the privilege granted to the convicts in such prisons as are under the direction of *justice* alone, that is to say, an intercourse with each other[BST], the means of conversing and forming connexions, which the necessity of other situations may excuse, even between the honest man and one of an opposite character, but which in the Bastille might often be founded on reciprocal esteem; though they would still be sensible of their distress, yet would they become the more capable of supporting it. There are certain liquors, which when separately taken are disgusting, but when mixed are rendered more agreeable to the palate. It is the same with misfortunes. But it is precisely this amalgamation of sighs, that the officers of the Bastille are so assiduous to prevent; what a prisoner might contrive to diminish of his sorrows, would be so much retrenched from their enjoyments. They might aptly take for a device, Caligula's address to the executioners whom he employed: *Strike so as to make him feel his death!*

[BST] The right to talk with other prisoners varied somewhat over time, but was also a function of a prisoner's status. In the seventeenth century, Cardinal de Retz was shocked that a number of prisoners had (he claims) as much freedom as the governor. Not only was he able to visit them, he conspired with some, meeting with them several times. Retz, Book I. Madame de Staal writes early on of the measures taken to ensure prisoners did not see each other, but she later managed to carry on an affair with one man and to be propositioned by at least one other. People also met in her apartment, to the point even of putting her in ill humor. Staal, 379, 431-432, 437-439. The notorious Count de Cagliostro used to walk on the very tower where, unknown to him, his wife was held. *Bastille devoilée*, II, 68, cited in *Mémoires de la Bastille*, 109n. Several prisoners had one or more roommates, sometimes quite a few in succession. Bucquoy and Latude – the castle's two most famous escapees – both worked with others to plan their escapes. Dumouriez was kept separate for a long time from his two servants, and found them depressing once they joined him. Dumouriez, II, 289-90.

From the moment a man is delivered into their hands, he is lost, as I observed before, to the whole universe: he *exists* only for them; for *they* are no less careful to prevent all correspondence within among their victims, than they are to exclude all communication from without. *La Porte,* and others, speak of an intercourse which they *had* with each other, by means of chimneys, &c.

Again let me observe, that it might have been the case in their time; but at present the tunnels of the chimneys are traversed, like the windows, by three iron grates, one above another; the first of which is at the distance of three feet from the hearth; and the mouths of the chimneys are raised several feet above the roof: The privies, a very rare accommodation, for I believe there are only two rooms in the whole *prison* provided with them[BST], are secured with the same kind of grating: many of the rooms are vaulted; the others are covered with a double ceiling.

When they think proper to order a prisoner downstairs,

[BST] Dumouriez at one point was in one of these, the chapel room, considered an especially good room:. He said it had "the privy outside". Dumouriez, II, 288. Perhaps Bucquoy was in the same room. He found his facilities handy in planning his famous escape: "....he resolved to find his salvation in the privies, at the risk of plunging into fecal matter. The commodities of this room were on the ditch of the St. Antoine Gate. This was the luckiest thing in the world, except for the odor." Du Noyer, 130. Improbable as it seems, this may have in fact been an opening built into the (very thick) walls: "Near the door, a smaller one led to latrines built into the thickness of the wall." Savine, 164. Bournon says: "To almost all of the rooms of the castle was annexed, in the thickness of the wall, a nook serving as a privy." Bournon, 145. La Porte, in the seventeenth century, says he only had a *terrine* (an earthenware chamber-pot). He later says it was emptied by a soldier on the steps – meaning (one hopes) out the window from the steps? La Porte, 356, 371. Most lists of furniture mention chamber-pots or close-stools (the French "pierced chair" – a seat with a hole in it.). In one case, a chamber-pot was used as a weapon. Savine, 36, 154. In 1783, an order for furniture included "twenty-four chairs for commodes". Bournon, 299. Not every prisoner confined his needs to his chamber-pot. Renneville, horrified by the filth of his new room in the Bertaudière tower, was told that the previous prisoner had habitually urinated against the walls. Savine, 62.

whether for an interrogatory, if he be so fortunate as to obtain one or to attend the Physician, if not so ill as to be under the necessity of being visited in his cell; or for the sham exercise of a walk, which I shall notice presently; or merely through the caprice of the Governor; he finds all silent, desert and obscure. The dismal croaking of the turn-key, by whom he is guided, serves as a signal for all to disappear, who might either see, or be seen by him. The windows of that part of the building where the principal officers hold their latent residence, of the kitchens, and of those parts where strangers are admitted, shield themselves instantly with curtains, lattices and blinds; and they have the cruelty not to proceed to this operation till he is in a situation to perceive it. Every thing is thus calculated to remind him, that within a few paces of him there are men; such perhaps as it would be the highest gratification for him to see, since they are so extremely anxious to conceal them: so that the torture is increasing in proportion to his curiosity; his agonies are multiplied in proportion to his attachments.

For a long time I imagined, that I had for a fellow-prisoner, a Person whose safety who alone would have been a solace sufficient to counterbalance all my other misfortunes, and whose apprehension, had they been able to effect it, would have been the completion of them. The answers that my interrogatories on this head extorted, were calculated only to confirm my suspicions: for these refiners on the art of tormenting, never fail, when they can find an opportunity, to blend an habitual silence, which puzzles and distracts you, with a simulated sincerity, which drives you to despair; whether they speak or are silent, you are sure to suffer no less from their freedom than from their reserve.

It is by these manœuvres that father and son, husband and wife, nay a whole parentage, may at once be inhabitants of the Bastille, without so much as suspecting themselves to be surrounded by objects so dear to them; or may languish there in the persuasion, that one common distress invelops the whole race, though a part may have been fortunate enough to escape it. When a Governor of St. Domingue took in his head, a few years back, to rid himself one morning of the Courts of justice, and to pack all the officers together in a vessel for France, immediately on their arrival, this whole American Parliament were lodged in the Bastille[BST].

There these poor men found the servitude more oppressive than that of their own negroes: their confinement lasted eight months; during which not one knew what was become of the others. At length they were tried, and declared innocent: and all the indemnification they got, was permission to return, and resume their employments!

But if they are so careful to hinder the captives from having the slightest knowledge of each other, they are not so scrupulous of making them acquainted that they are not alone in misfortune. Those double floors, those vaulted roofs, impervious to consolation, are sure indexes to point out to the wretched prisoner, that there is, above or below him, another wretch, whose condition is no less lamentable than his own. The doors, the keys, the bolts, are not silent: the creaking of the first, the clattering of the second, and the hollow jarring of the last, resound from afar along those flights of stone that form the stair-case, and echo dreadfully in the vast vacuity of the towers. Hence it was easy for me to compute the number of my neighbors: and this was a fresh source of sorrowful reflexion.

To be sensible that you have over your head, or under your feet, an afflicted being, on whom you might confer, or with whom you might participate, comfort; to hear him walk

---

[BST] This must be one of the very few – if not unique - cases when anyone was sent overseas expressly to be put in the Bastille. Ravaisson succinctly resumes the affair: "The inhabitants [of Saint Domingue]...offered to pay the administration four million to support colonial battalions, in the place of the militia which was suppressed March 24, 1763... but, in 1768, a royal statute reestablished this hated institution, while nonetheless demanding the tax of four million....The chevalier de Rohan, governor of this colony, sent the statute to the council in Port-au-Prince to be registered: this was to require it to consecrate a breaking of one's word and a brazen theft; the councilors, instead of obeying, protested. M. de Rohan sent them to France." Ravaisson, Tome 19, 450. Though he also gives a racial breakdown of the militias in question, he does not specify if any of the councilors sent to France were of mixed race. If so, that too would have been a rarity in the castle's history.

lightly; to reflect that he is but three feet distant: to consider the pleasure there would be in breaking through that narrow space, together with the impossibility of effecting it; to have cause for affliction, no less from the bustle that announces the arrival of a newcomer, who is to partake of, without alleviating your bondage, than from the silence of the dungeons, that gives you notice of the happier lot of your former companions in misery, are punishments beyond what the imagination can conceive: they are those of Tantalus, Ixion, and Sisyphus, united[10].

But this anxiety is sometimes still more horrible. I am convinced that my fellow-captive in the chamber below mine died during my imprisonment; though I cannot say whether. his death was natural, or inflicted. It happened, one morning about two o'clock, that I heard a prodigious uproar upon the stair-case: a vast number of people were ascending the stairs in a tumultuous manner, and advanced no farther than the door of that chamber: they seemed there to be engaged in much bustle and dispute, and to be running frequently backwards and forward! I heard very distinctly repeated struggles and groans.

Now was this an act of succor, or an assassination? Was it the introduction of a Physician, or an Executioner? I know not: but three days after, about the same hour in the morning; I heard, at the same door, a nose less violent. I thought I could distinguish the carrying up, the setting down, the filling, and the shutting of a coffin: these ceremonies were succeeded by a strong smell of juniper[11]. In another place these proceedings would not have caused so much alarm, but judge what an impression must they not have made, *in the Bastille;* at such an hour, and at so small a distance!

Sharp objects: suicide and shaving

Whilst the regimen of the Bastille places by these means, and by others which I shall advert to presently, the life of everyone thrown into it, in the hands of his keepers; it will also have his fate dependent on them alone. They are conscious, and it is one of their principal enjoyments, that their regimen is productive of nothing but despair: they are well aware, that there are moments, when such in particular of their victims, as have not had their courage awed by crimes, or their sensibility enervated by habitual knavery, would be tempted to put an end, by a transitory pang, to so tedious a succession of agonies: and that is precisely what they labour to prevent. They are even more apprehensive lest one of their captives should evade the torments they inflict on him, by death, than by any escape. This *Phalaris* of a Governor is, above all, anxious that his prisoners may feel to the utmost the fiery tortures of his *bull*[21]; and, by an art peculiar to the Bastille, the multifarious precautions, which they adopt in order to obviate this pretended danger, are no less humiliating than painful; are as fit to foment a desire of the catastrophe which they are calculated to prevent, as they are to hinder the execution of it.

I observed that a prisoner was not permitted to have scissors, knife, or razors[BST]. Thus, when they serve him with *provisions,* repelled by his sighs and watered by his tears, it is

---

[BST] Even today, it is no more unusual for prisons to ban sharp objects than it is for prisoners to creatively circumvent such rules. In the Bastille, this was another restriction that seems to have tightened over time. When Renneville lists his first meal setting (1701), he mentions "a spoon and tin fork, a little knife" and even then asks if "the governor took me for a bandit to send me a spoon and a fork of tin." Savine, 36. Marmontel, in 1759, got only a spoon and a fork (of silver), as did his valet (of tin), though he was treated overall with the greatest consideration. Marmontel, II, 133-134. When shaving a prisoner, the surgeon-major of the castle was to take out only the razor needed and to carefully close his case. Bournon, 274. Still, special permission could be granted. Sartine did not outright forbid a prisoner's request for a knife, razor and scissors, but referred the request to a higher authority. Ravaisson, Tome 18, 42. The prison's famous escapees did what they could to get around these limits. Bucquoy used a classic hiding place for prisoners to keep a blade: "the Abbé determined to use his body as a reserve...he had a small blade which he had always hidden with care and which had escaped the vigilance of those who had searched him more than once." He also improvised tools from "bits of iron, copper plates, nails and knife blades" which he'd gathered in his different rooms and sharpened on his pitcher and hardened in the fire. Du Noyer, 134, 156. Latude describes how he used an iron chandelier to make a pen knife which served him as a saw in preparing for his escape. Masers de Latude, 60.

necessary that the Turn-key cut every morsel for him. For this purpose he makes use of a knife rounded at the point, which he is careful to put up in his pocket, after each dissection.

One cannot prevent the nails from shooting out, or the hair from growing. But a prisoner has no means of getting rid of these incumbrances without undergoing fresh humiliation: he must request the loan of a pair of scissors; the Turn-key stands by while he is using them, and carries them off immediately after.

As to the beard, it is the Surgeon's business to shave; and this office he performs twice a week[BST2]. He and the Turn--key, Agent, or Super-intendant to all that passes in the Tower, carefully watch that the hand of the prisoner does not approach too near the formidable instrument: like the axe of the Executioner, it is developed only at the moment of using it. They still remember, in the Bastille, the disturbance occasioned there by the temerity of Mr. *Lally;* though at a time when he little suspected his impending fate. He one day got hold of a razor, and in a jocular manner refused to give it up[BST]. That did not indicate any very desperate design; ne-

---

[BST2] This was an improvement on earlier years. By the time he had his beard cut for the first time, says Renneville, "my beard served as my cravate". Later, he again found himself with a long beard. In terms of personal hygiene, worse was to come: he was refused washing water at one point and had to use his own urine and saliva. Under one regime, the surgeon (also a barber, as was often true in earlier times) demanded 30 sols to shave each beard (but came in with a magnificent set-up). Savine, 82, 104, 162, 171. Berville and Barrière quote a prisoner's request to be shaven after two weeks in the Bastille (1756) as proof that special permission was needed, at least at that point. *Mémoires de Linguet,* 78n.

[BST] The administration's concern was not totally unwarranted. When he heard his sentence of execution (at the Conciergerie), General Lally tried to kill himself by plunging a compass point, brought from the Bastille, four inches into his chest. *Biographie universelle,* XXII, 648. A fellow prisoner of Bucquoy's "cut his veins" in a sham suicide meant to hurry his release (which it did). Du Noyer, 142. When Dumouriez asked why his shoe buckles were being confiscated, he was told that a prisoner had killed himself in swallowing the tongues of his buckles. He notes wryly: "After this lovely remark, the major had the horrible imprudence to leave [me]

vertheless the alarm-bell resounded through out the castle. The guard was put under arms, and twenty bayonets pointed toward the chamber: perhaps they were even preparing the cannon; when peace was restored by the return of the dreadful tool into its case.

It is futile and ridiculous to urge the pretence, that this circumspection of theirs has for its object the security of the keepers, no less than that of the captives. What can be dreaded from a man loaded with such heavy chains, hemmed in by so many walls, encompassed by so many guards, and watched with so much attention? But whatever their motive for being afraid to leave him so miserable a resource, it is evident that it is despair they are the most apprehensive of. Now they know that this despair is the consequence only of their own re-iterated tortures; and they disarm his hands, merely to have it in their power to rend his heart with impunity.

Turn-keys

I have often mentioned the *Turn-keys*, without explaining the nature of their office. They are the subaltern officers of the castle, and have charge of all that relates to the service of the prisoners. This indeed is but trifling; for all they have to do is, to distribute the provisions throughout the cages within their respective districts. They visit them thrice a day, at seven o'clock in the morning, at eleven, and at six in the afternoon: those are the hours of breakfast, of dinner and supper[BST]. They are closely watched, lest they should make a longer stay than is requisite to deposit their burthen: thus in the twenty-four ages that compose a day, or rather a night, in the Bastille, a prisoner has but there three short reliefs.

---

the buckles of [my] garters." (He later used the tongue from one as an improvised writing tool). Dumouriez, II, 257-258, 268.
[BST] The subject of meals at the Bastille is a rich one - see Appendix C.

The turn-keys are not even required to make the beds, or to sweep out the rooms[BST2]. The reason assigned for it, is, that in the execution of this business they might be ill-treated, or perhaps assassinated. The justice of this pretext admits an enquiry; the thing itself is certain. Neither age, nor infirmity, nor delicacy of sex, can exempt the prisoners from this necessity; the man of letters, unaccustomed to these operations, and the opulent man no less unacquainted with them, are equally obliged to submit to the same etiquette.

The turn-keys indeed do not invariably conform to it: they sometimes render services that cannot be exacted of them[BST3]. But they must do it with as much secrecy, as if they were holding an illicit correspondence with an enemy; the Fury disguised in the form of a Governor, who will take the alarm if he cannot hear, as he passes the dungeon, the groans or lamentations of his captives, would quickly punish them for their ill-timed lenity.

Lack of diversion

It is in this total silence, I must again repeat it, in this general desolation, in this void a silence more cruel than death, since it does not exclude grief, but rather engenders every kind of grief; it is in this universal abomination, it cannot be repeated too often, that what is called a Prisoner of State in the Bastille, that is, a man who has displeased a Minister a Clerk in office, or a Valet, is given up without resource, without any other diversion but his own thoughts

---

[BST2] But they were, in theory, obliged to clean the toilets. A list of duties (from around 1764) says they are to "clean the prisoners' commodes well every day." Bournon, 291.

[BST3] Renneville says they also took tips: "One turn-key, leaving here, bought a good piece of land for 80,000 francs with an estate that lets him live like a great lord."; "All the officers and especially the turn-keys did very well." But he then says that under the next governor, several were punished severely for accepting money to do favors for the prisoners. In a note to Renneville's account, Savine says they were not to accept any gratifications "except at [the prisoner's] departure." Ru, a turn-key who was generally considered kind, complained bitterly that one prisoner only gave him three louis when he left. "A reasonable prisoner, when he leaves here, gives at the very least thirty louis." Savine, 51, 101-102.

or his alarms, to the most bitter sentiment that can agitate a heart yet undegraded by criminality,: that of oppressed innocence, which foresees its destruction without, the possibility of a vindication; it is thence that he may fruitlessly implore the succor of the laws, the communication of what he is accused of, the interference of his friends: his prayers, his supplications, his groans are not only uttered in vain; but even acknowledged by his tyrants to be useless: and this is the only information they vouchsafe him. Abandoned to all the horror of listlessness, of inaction, he is daily sensible of the approaching close of his existence; and he is at the same time sensible, that they prolong it only to prolong his punishment. Derision and insult are added to cruelty, in order to increase the bitterness of privation.

For instance, at the end of about eight months, I conceived the idea of eluding the tedious hours of my confinement by a recollection of my past mathematical studies. I accordingly applied for a case of instruments; and took care to limit the size to three inches, in order to obviate all pretext of a refusal. This favour I was obliged to solicit for the space of two months; perhaps a Cabinet Council was convened to consider of it. It was at length granted: the case arrived-but without compass. On signifying my disappointment at it, they informed me coolly that *arms* are prohibited in the Bastille.

I had to sollicit afresh, to petition, to memorialize, to discuss seriously the difference between a mathematical case of instruments and a cannon. After another month, thanks to the charity and to the invention of the Commissary, the compasses were brought. But in what fashion?———made of bone. Of such substance had they fabricated, at my expence, all that in a case of instruments should be made of steel.

I still preserve this new-fashioned piece of geometrical apparatus. After having kept it as the ornament of my study whilst I live, I shall be careful that after my death it shall be consigned to some magazine, or museum, where it may not be a at a loss for spectators. It will there hold a distinguished place amidst the monuments of barbarian industry, of which travellers sometimes favour us with a sample. No invention of the most ingenious among the savage tribes can be more deservedly an object of public curiosity.

Rates and revenues

In consequence of that principle, that the man, on whom the King, or rather, the Minister, has thus laid his hand, must become invisible without redemption, they have resolved that the existence of the prisoners should be confided in the hands of those who are employed to secrete them; in order to render their underhand, clandestine practices confidential. The Governor finds them in provision by contract, and gains an immense profit by a kind of regal sixpenny ordinary.

Government has founded fifteen places in the Bastille, the salaries of which are paid, whether they are occupied or not at the rate of ten French livres, or eight shillings English *per diem*. Hence the Governor of the castle draws a revenue of near 2500l. *per annum*.

But that is not all: in drawing up a *Lettre-de-cachet*, which gives him a new Boarder, they add to the primitive foundation so much *per* head, proportioned to the quality of each respective rank. Thus, a Plebeian, or one the lowest order, brings to the general mess, over and above the pistole[13] allowed on the establishment, half a crown extraordinary *per diem*; a Tradesman, or Civilian of the ordinary class, four shillings; a Priest, a Financier, or a common Judge, eight shillings; a Counselor in Parliament, twelve shillings; a Lieutenant-General in the army, a Guinea; and a Marshall of France, a Guinea and a half. In this Ministerial *cadastre*[*], I know not the government rate allotted for a Prince of the Blood Royal[BST].

---

[*] *Cadastra*, Public Register for the assessment of the land-tax, particularly in Provence, Dauphiny, and Languedoc. It corresponds to the *Census* among the Romans, and to our Domes-day Book. It has here the sense of *quota*, or proportion. [*Original translator's note*]
[BST] For a prince of the blood, the amount was fifty Tournois pounds. Berville and Barrière point out that this list must date from after 1692,

They have, besides, granted to the Governor the privilege of stowing in his vaults near an hundred buts of wine free of all duties. This is no inconsiderable object, and, it should seem, would render it the easier for him to provide for his lodgers in a handsome manner.

But let us see how far it is attended with such effect. He sells this indemnity to a Publican of Paris, named *Joli*, for two hundred and fifty pounds sterling; and takes in exchange the very worst kind of wines, for the prisoners' consumption; which wine we may fully suppose, is no better than vinegar. He considers the establishment of eight shillings *per* day as part of the income attached to his office, which he is to give no account of, and which has nothing to do with the reckoning on the head of subsistence[BST2]. On this he employs only the extraordinary surplus, which the liberality of the Sovereign destined merely to augment it; and this very surplus he is careful not entirely to expend. The detail of these particulars is farther ignoble: nevertheless, it is extremely requisite, they be made known, There are prisoners in the Bastille, who at a meal are not allowed above four ounces of meat. These portions have been weighed more than once. The inferior Officers know the fact, and lament it. (5) Nothing could be more easily verified, if the Minister would shield from the resentment of their chief, the Subalterns who might disclose his sordid peculation.

There were some tables, indeed, better supplied; and mine, I allow, was of the humbler[BST]. But is this abundance a

---

since it counts one crown (*écu*) for a peddler, but a peddler complains on that date that only 4 sous are allocated for his expenses. *Mémoires de Linguet*, 85-86n. Bournon disputes some of Linguet's figures and says that the exceptional rates were rarely granted. Bournon, 55.

[BST2] "Even taking into account the familiar exaggerations of Linguet, it is certain that this privilege was lucrative." Bournon, 56-57.

[BST] I must contradict the original translator here. The French original means, literally, "There are tables less lacking; I confess it; mine was of their number." (*"Il y a des tables moins denuées; je l'avoue; la mienne était du nombre."*) That is, far from saying his table was one of the 'humbler', Linguet is (begrudgingly) admitting he was decently fed.

good, or an evil, to those whom it is granted? This is a question I cannot answer with precision. Though it carries, a more honourable appearance, perhaps it may conceal some dangerous artifice. I have known several who during *their* confinement in the Bastille have lived on milk alone: others, as Mr. *De la Bourdonnaie,* have solicited and obtained permission to be served with provisions from their own houses[BST2]. They constantly refused me this privilege, and even, for the first eight months, that of buying any article whatever, as I have already observed, although I had money deposited in the hands of the Officers.

Fear of poisoning

I made amends for this, by the most scrupulous attention to eat but little of every dish; to wash several times whatever had a suspicious appearance: yet, notwithstanding all these precautions, I could not entirely escape what I dreaded with too much reason[BST3]. The eighth day of my confinement I was seized with a cholic and a vomiting of blood, to which I was afterwards ever subject; a disorder, of which the reiterated attacks indicated the frequent renewal of the cause.

On this subject I was neither doubtful nor silent. I wrote an hundred times to the Lieutenant-General of the Police that

---

[BST2] Mahé de la Bourdonnaie (see note above) did have this privilege but lost it when he used it to smuggle information. *Mémoires de Linguet,* 218.

[BST3] This accusation seems to be pure exaggeration. No source consulted here mentions a prisoner being murdered outright, though Bucquoy too thought (very briefly) he was being poisoned. Du Noyer, 148. On the other hand, at least one prisoner did kill a guard, in 1688, using a bar from his bed. *Mémoires de Linguet,* 208. Berville and Barrière do say, of reading through comments by the staff, "If nothing suggests [they] were capable of crimes, nothing suggests either that they had very exalted natures, nor much humanity." *Ibid,* 172n. La Harpe – a frequent target of Linguet's attacks – responded wryly to Linguet's claim, though he began by acknowledging the arbitrary and illegal nature of the Bastille: "Anyone whose been put in the Bastille has the right to complain.. But who does Linguet think will believe that they wanted to poison him…. By his own account…it is sure that any man they wanted to get rid of would soon be annihilated without leaving the least trace of his existence. If Linguet is alive, it is because they did not want to kill him." *Correspondance Littéraire,* IV, 118-119.

they were giving me potion. I declared the same thing verbally to his substitute; I declared it to the Physician, to the Surgeon, to the officers themselves, of the Castle: all the answer I could ever get was an insulting laugh.

"If they wished to poison you, how comes it that you are still alive?" many persons have said, when I recounted these extraordinary symptoms; and the same objections may now perhaps be suggested by my readers: but a little reflection will quickly do it way. No, most assuredly; I never could have survived the murderers design, had it been that of Government, of the Minister: but my present existence, which I impute to the strength of my constitution justifies him alone. Can we suppose the hands, which would be ready to execute so base a villainy, if he was capable of requiring it, would have virtue to resist; a lucrative solicitation from another quarter?

By the unaccountable regimen, of which we are speaking, nothing that may serve either to amuse or to console a prisoner is allowed to approach him; but whatever may contribute either to afflict his mind or to injure his health, finds no such difficulty of admittance. There are four officers of the higher order; the inferior order consists of our Turnkeys, and the kitchen is provided with the same number of Cooks or Scullions. These twelve persons are well informed whom they serve, notwithstanding the ridiculous affectation, with which it is pretended to keep them in ignorance of it: they are all permitted to go out, and to mix every day with the inhabitants of the city: there they have houses, wives, friends. acquaintance. Is it so difficult a matter, then, to find a single villain in a society whose office is but a tissue of flagitious actions? or is it more so for him, who is once suborned, to discern what parties to give the mortal blow to, since he is not denied access to any? But we cannot suppose them capable of such horrid barbarity! Could we suppose them capable of those already described?

So far is this danger from being imaginary, that they formerly posted in the kitchen a sentinel, whose business it was to examine, and keep account of all who approached the fire-places, or the stoves. This precaution, still more salutary than offensive, has for some years back been omitted: are the evil designs, the practibility of which it clearly indicated, become more difficult to perpetrate?

That, of which I was the object, was not consummated: but the loudness of my complaints might have disconcerted the plan, and my cares in part may have rendered it fruitless. I do not mean to suggest, that all those to whom I revealed my suspicions on this head, were accomplices in the crime by which they were occasioned. The real guilty person was perhaps afraid to verify too quickly my apprehensions, less an enquiry should be the result of it. The habitual weakness under which I languished, the imminent danger was in at the close of 1781. My death being then considered as inevitable, might have induced them to relax in their endeavours, and to think all attempts of that tendency superfluous.

But even supposing I was mistaken in the cause I assumed for events, the illness of which I still carry about me; allowing these apprehensions and symptoms to have been merely the product of an imagination disordered through too much susceptibility; is it not shocking that the confinement of the Bastille should be calculated to produce fears of that nature, by rendering it impossible for a prisoner to avoid those secret machinations which give rise to the dread he labours under?

After all, this dispute is merely verbal. I will admit, that in a place, where the Italian $Exili^{BST}$ (6) kept about a century ago a school for poisoning, they have not preserved any one of his receipts; and that a single additional cruelty may be repugnant to men, whose office, I repeat again, is the continual perpetration of cruelties: but will not a residence of

---

[BST] (Nicolo? or Antonio?) Exili (possibly Egidi or Eggidio) — He is best known, on scant evidence, as a master poisoner who played an indirect part in the Affair of the Poisons, one of the great scandals of Louis XIV's reign. He supposedly shared a cell with and taught Godin de Sainte-Croix, lover and accomplice of the Marquise de Brinvilliers (the prime figure in that scandal.) But the archives do not confirm their sharing a cell (Exili was there from 2/2/1663 to 6/27/1663, Sainte-Croix from 3/19/1663 to 5/2/1663.) Ravaisson, Tome 4, 1-2.

twenty months, with all its concomitant evils, in a place where existence is but a repetition of tortures worse than death, essentially impair the source of life? Will near two years passed in these dungeons, without air, without exercise, in all the horrors of listlessness, in all the anguish of suspence, or rather of despair, make less impression on the vital organs than the most efficacious poison? It may be slower: but is it less certain? Between these two methods of destroying, what difference is there but the time?

Tours for visitors

But are they totally deprived of air and exercise, say they who have read the ancient accounts of the Bastille, and even they whose curiosity has led them to visit it? For it is not withdrawn from the inspection of the curious. The Governor, although his mansion is without, often enters the prison to receive his visitors: and in the prison all his colleagues, from the King's Lieutenant down to the very lowest Scullion, receive theirs. On days of rejoicing when there is a display of fire-works or illuminations, the public are permitted even in crouds to ascend the Towers, that they may thence behold the sight to advantage. On such occasions they reflect the very image of peace and tranquility. All these gaping strangers are in perfect ignorance of what passes, and of what is shut up, within those impenetrable vaults, the outsides of which they gaze in with admiration. Some one amongst them perhaps may tread on the sepulcher of his friend, his relation, his father, who thinks him two hundred leagues distant employed in his business, or engaged in his pleasures.

All, in short, who are favoured with this exterior examination, seeing a garden pretty large, platforms raised to a considerable elevation, where in consequence the air is pure and the view picturesque, and being assured that all this in common allotted to the use of the prisoners, leave the Castle, fully persuaded, though the life in the Bastille may not be agreeable, yet that these alleviations render it supportable, This might have been the case formerly: I shall mention a fact that has happened lately.

Limits on exercise

The present Governor, named *De Launay*[BST], is an ingenious man, and knows how to turn every thing to the best advantage; he considered, that the garden might afford a handsome addition to his income; and for this purpose let it out for a certain annual stipend to a Gardener, who sells the roots and fruit that it produces: but, in order to make the better bargain, he thought it necessary to exclude the prisoners. A letter was therefore expedited, signed *Amelot*[14], which prohibited the prisoners from entering the garden.

With regard to the platforms of the Towers, though from their great elevation, it is impossible for anyone to be recognized on them, or for him to recognize anyone below; yet as they directly overlook the *Rue St. Antoine*, from which the public are not yet banished, prisoners were never permitted heretofore to walk there, unless escorted by one of the jailors, either an officer or turn-key[BST]. It was, however, discovered of late, that is, within these three years, that this task was both unprofitable and toilsome; besides, that it afforded the prisoners an opportunity of conversing with the sentry. The vigilance of Mr. *De Launay* took the alarm: and partly in consideration of the ease of his colleagues, partly on

---

[BST] Bernard René Jourdan, Marquis de Launay (1740-1789). The last governor of the Bastille, he was born there (when his father was governor), and was murdered after surrendering the castle. ("Bastille." *Encyclopædia Britannica*.) He became governor in October 1776. Linguet's less than objective remarks on him nonetheless seem accurate: "[A] proud and stupid despot", one author calls him. "As soon he arrived, the most severe, the most tyrannical regime was established at the Bastille for everybody; hard and haughty towards employees, brutal, arbitrary and hateful towards the prisoners, he added... a thousand deprivations, a thousand cruelties to a captivity already so painful." Arnould, VI, 158.

[BST] La Porte contradicts the idea that people below could not recognize prisoners above. His loyalty to the Queen, Anne of Austria, had led to his arrest. One day while walking outside, he says, he saw her step out of her carriage below and wave to him in approval of his conduct. La Porte, 380-381. Later Madame de Staal, who had been allowed walks on the towers, was suddenly forbidden them on the grounds that she might signal to people below. Her protest that she was near-sighted were to no avail. She entered the garden during this talk and said - quoting Racine's *Phèdre* (Act I, Scene III) -: "Sun, I come to see you for the last time". Staal, 395.

account of the dangers he apprehended, a letter was dispatched, signed *Amelot,* which forbad the use of the platforms, as well as the garden.

All that remains then for walking in, is the Court of the castle. This is an oblong square, ninety-fix feet by sixty. The walls, by which it is surrounded, are one hundred feet high, without any aperture: so that it is in fact a large pit, where the cold is insupportable in winter, because the North wind rushes into it; in summer it is no less so, because, there being no circulation of the air, the heat of the Sun makes it a very oven. Such is the sole *Lyceum*[15], where those among the prisoners, who are indulged with the privilege of walking, a privilege that is not granted to all, may for a few moments of the day disgorge the infected air of their habitations.

But it must not be supposed, that the act of tormenting, with which they keep their captives in misery, is suffered to relax during this transitory interval: for it may easily be conceived, how little they can enjoy walking in a place so circumscribed; where there is no shelter from the rain; where nothing but the inconveniencies of the weather is experienced; where with the appearance of a shadow of liberty, the centinels that surround them, the universal silence that prevails, and the sight of the clock, which is alone allowed to break that silence, present them with but too certain marks of slavery.

Chained figures on the clock

This particular may be worthy of a remark. The Clock of the Castle looks into the Court. It is covered with a handsome dial-plate; but, who would imagine the ornaments with which they have thought proper to decorate it? Chains carved with much exactness, and highly finished. It is supported by two figures, bound by the hands, the feet and the waist: the two ends of this curious garland, after being carried all round the plate, return to form a prodigious knot in front; and, to signify that they menace both sexes alike, the Artist either inspired by the genius of the place, or else in pursuance of precise directions, has carefully made the distinction of a *male* and a *female*[BST]. Such is the spectacle, with which the eyes of a prisoner are regaled during the eyes of a prisoner are regaled during the walk: a large inscription in letters of gold engraved on black marble informs that he is indebted for to M. *Raymond Gualbert de* SARTINES. (7)

Yet do not imagine, that he enjoys so much of this as he could desire. The portion of time that is allotted to each prisoner to view the sky, which he can do but in part, is measured out with the most œconomical exactness. This measure depends on the number of the confined. As one never enters till another is gone out, and so, thanks to the letters signed *Amelot*, this is the only funnel they are allowed to partake of, when the Bastille is full, the portion is very small. I perceived the arrival of a new guest, or of a new walker, by what was deducted from mine to contribute to his recreation[BST2].

The "closet"

But observe that you are not carried are away with the erroneous idea, that the enjoyment of this relief, thus modified, is peaceable and complete. This Court is the only passage to the kitchen, and to those parts where the Officers of the Castle receive their visitors; through it the purveyors of every kind, the work men, &c. are obliged to pass. Now, as it is requisite, above all things, that a prisoner neither see, nor be seen; whenever a stranger approaches, he is obliged to fly into what is called the *closet*. This is an opening of twelve feet in length, and two wide, made in an ancient vault. To this hole, which they term the *closet,* a prisoner must betake himself with precipitation on the approach of so much as a man with a bundle of herbs; and he must be scrupulously careful to shut and fasten the door; for the smallest suspicion of curiosity would at least be punished with close

---

[BST] Coeuret says both figures were male, one younger than the other. He also says that when the Prime Minister Breteuil heard about this passage in Linguet's work, he immediately had the images of chains removed. Coeuret, 32.

[BST2] The Abbé Morellet, confirming this, says that he gave up his exercise time when he realized it took away from that of others. I, 98.

imprisonment. This alternative will frequently occur: I have often reckoned in an hour, the term of duration for the longest walk, three quarters of the hour consumed in that inactive and humiliating situation in the *closet*.

I know not whether this regulation is established by a letter signed *Amelot*; but sure I am, that it is of a recent date. Till of late years, no stranger was admitted into the Court after nine in the morning, without the most indispensable necessity: the provisions were ready prepared; visits were paid without; and the manœuvres of the *closet* took place only on such occasions as might from their urgency seem to excuse it.

But that is not all: this walk itself, so insufficient, and so cruelly modified, as to be rendered rather an additional mortification, than a comfort, is suspended daily; and that by the arbitrary will of the Governor. If a curious person has obtained permission to visit the prison, if any repairs require the passage backward and forward of the workmen; if the Governor gives a grand dinner, which must occasion the frequent passage of his servants, his kitchen being within, and his dwelling without; for any one of these reasons the walk is prohibited[BST].

In 1781, during the hot weather for which that summer was remarkable, labouring under a vomiting of blood, oppressed by the heat of the season, and by a weakness of stomach though not occasioned yet fomented by it, I passed the whole months of July and August, without being suffered to quit my chamber. The pretext was, a work that was going forward upon the platforms. Yet the workmen might easily have ascended on the outside; and they did in fact ascend that way: all that it was necessary to convey through the court was the stone and other materials. This operation might have been done, as formerly, every morning before nine o'clock. But M. *De Launay* thought that would be rather troublesome: it appeared much easier for him to, say *Let there be no walking!* and there was none.

[BST] The old kitchens were in the building in the courtyard. Later a new building with a kitchen and baths was built just outside the main castle, across from the governor's house. See Appendix B.

In order to form an idea of the anguish of this privation, we must consider, that it is the last they can put in force to rack their prisoner; we must reflect, that it not only exposes him to physical inconvenience, and necessarily impairs his health; but that the motion of the body being the sole expedient to assuage the convulsions of the mind, by taking away that resource these are rendered the more poignant; that when he has not a single minute in the day to vary at least the nature of his torment, his heart ever heaving with sighs seems to beat with more pungent grief, and with stronger pulsations, against the walls with which it is environed on every side.

More on secret custody

Thus in the prisons belonging to the ordinary courts of justice this rigour is considered as the most severe it is allowed to inflict on criminals, previous to their conviction. A *secret* custody, or absolute seclusion takes place only in those short intervals, during which the prisoner might derive from without, information repugnant to the execution of the laws. The motive for this concealment may be the particular situation of places, or a regard to humanity, which leaving the prisoners a free and open communication permits the suspension in a single instance, by banishing one prisoner from the society of the rest, for as long a time only as the motive for this suspension may last: it becomes indeed necessary to prohibit the privilege to one, in order to preserve it to all the others.

And, besides, this temporary inaction is much alleviated, particularly if he is innocent, by the preparations for his trial. He sees his judges, his accusers, his witnesses; he knows the charges against him[16]. Whether they confront him, or only interrogate him, he has the satisfaction of not being alone; and whenever one of these conflicts is at an end, the intermediate solitude becomes precious, and even necessary to prepare for a second.

But, in the Bastille, not one of these motives, or of these

solaces, can be admitted. The *secret custody* is there perpetual: all a prisoner's walks are solitary as his mansion: they can neither be an impediment to the trial, when resolved on nor to the means or facility of conviction This being the case, to step in with an arbitrary prohibition; to deprive a prisoner of the power of raising, for a few minutes in the day, his eyes swollen with tears, to the sun, which seems to avoid him, is the excess no less of injustice, than of cruelty.

What then shall we say, when no trial is intended; when this prohibition falls on men, against whom hatred and vengeance cannot even find the pretext for an arraignment; when it is kept in force for months together; when it is kept in force for months together; when it depends on the caprice of a Satellite; whose baseness is equaled only by his barbarity; who, puffed up with the privilege of committing in his fortress outrages on men of worth and distinction with impunity, thinks himself powerful in proportion as he torments them, and honourable as he insults them in their affliction?

It may be urged, that these particulars apply rather to the character of the persons appointed to preside, than to the fundamental constitution of the prison. True: but it is of itself sufficiently severe, without receiving an addition from the capricious tyranny of Governors: and it does receive that addition; for, as I have before observed, the barbarities of the Bastille have been much increased within these few years[BST]. Formerly, they endeavoured to guard their prisoners; now they strive to make a sport of their miseries.

[BST] While this may be yet another case of Linguet's self-centered evaluation of circumstances, the author of *La Bastille dévoilée* does suggest that treatments got worse over time because, originally, it was the king who sent enemies of the state to the Bastille, and that he was above all interested in locking them away. But, he says, as ministers and their friends began to have their enemies imprisoned (a premise which itself should not be accepted uncritically), they were more likely to feel personal rancor, and to have the prisoners treated accordingly. *La Bastille dévoilée*, II, 55, cited in *Mémoires de Linguet*, 6n.

And, what may seem very extraordinary, the additions, whether inhuman or scandalous, with which the present government have enriched a regimen already so scandalous and inhuman, they have extended even to the very mercenaries whom they employ. In former times, as I have already observed, the Officers of the superior order had a right to see singly, when they thought proper, the prisoner confided to their common vigilance. Being all reputed alike trusty, their particular visits gave neither cause for suspicion nor alarm: and, as there are four of them, there was often one to be found among them, whose heart was not so unsusceptible of pity, and who often consecrated some moments of the day to conversation every pleasing to those who partook of them.

This mark of condescension displeased the Ministry; and a letter came, signed as before, which prohibited the Officers from entering alone into the towers, and which required them to go at least two at a time, without including the Turn-key. The visits of the Physician are restricted to the same formality. These bull-dogs are no longer suffered to walk but in pairs.

This monkish regulation has produced the desired effect, that is a total discontinuance of visits. It is difficult to find in such a pack two souls equally susceptible. Besides, it would be necessary to have the matter preconcerted, and for them both to be ready at the same moment: moreover there is no intercourse of friendship between them: they are mutually jealous and diffident of each other: debased, even in their own eyes, by their abominable office, they tremble at the interpretations that might be affixed to the most simple expression: by the Adjunct, or rather the Spy, who must ever accompany them: finally, this innovation being an index of the increase of insensibility. Thus is this trivial consolation no longer to be met with in the Bastille; and it is only three years since it has been banished from it.

Illness

But with regard to the health of the prisoners, perhaps the reader may be curious to know what degree of attention they pay to it. *D'Argenson*[BST], Lieutenant of the *Police*, in a letter to *Madame de Maintenon*, concerning State-Prisons about the beginning of the present century, expresses himself in the following terms: "I can assure you that the prisoners have nothing to wish for in the articles of diet or cloathing (8): and I many add, that the Governors of the *Bastille* and *Vincennes* manifest towards theirs, a *charitable* attention, beyond what could be either required or expected: on every slight indisposition they afford them all the assistance, both spiritual and temporal, their condition will admit; but *the privation of liberty renders them insensible to every other benefit."* . . . . .

Although we may be permitted to express our surprise at the coalition of those two words, charity and the Bastille; though we may harbour our suspicions, from the indifference of the concluding phrase, that *M. D'Argenson* in speaking thus conformed to the language of a *Lieutenant of Police*, that is to say, of a man devoted by his office to barbarity, and interested in the justification of those to whom he is necessarily an accomplice; we may, notwithstanding, suppose, that there was *some* colour of truth in his assertions. If so, some things are vastly altered; and the fact will but serve to prove more fully the late augmentation of cruelty in a place where from the beginning it appeared to have arrived at the extreme height of depravation.

First, as to those transitory complaints or sudden attacks, which can only be obviated by ready assistance and immediate application, a prisoner must either be perfectly free from them, or must sink under them if they are severe; for it would be in vain to look for any immediate succour, particularly during the night. Each room is secured by two thick doors bolted and locked, both within and without; and each tower is fortified with one still stronger. The Turn-keys lie in a building entirely separate and at a considerable

---

[BST] Marc-René de Voyer d'Argenson (1652-1721). Named Lieutenant General of the Police in 1697, he organized the first true police force in Paris and an extensive network of spies as well. Savine, 38n.

distance: no voice can possibly reach them[BST].

The only resource left is to knock at the door: but will an apoplexy, or an hæmorrhage, leave a prisoner the ability to do it? It is even extremely doubtful, whether the Turn-keys would hear the knocking; or whether once lain down, they would think proper to hear it.

Those nevertheless, whom the disorder may not have deprived of the use of their legs and voice, have still one method left of applying for assistance. The ditch, with which the castle is surrounded, is only an hundred and fifty feet wide: on the brink of the opposite bank is placed a gallery, called the passage of the rounds; and on this gallery the sentinels are posted. The windows overlook the ditch; through them, therefore, the patient may cry out for succor: and if the interior grate, which repels his breath, as was before explained, is not carried too far into the chamber; if his voice is powerful; if the wind is moderate; if the centinel is not asleep, it is not impossible but he may be heard.

The Soldier must then cry the next sentry; and the alarm must circulate from one sentry to another, till it arrives at the guard-room. The Corporal then goes forth to see *what is the matter;* and, when informed from what window the cries issue, he returns back again the same way, (all which takes up no inconsiderable time) and passes through the gate into the interior of the prison. He then calls up one of the Turn-keys; and the Turn-key proceeds to call up the Lackey of the King's Lieutenant, who must also awaken his Master, in order to get the key: for all, without exception, are deposited every night at that officer's lodging. There is no garrison, where in time of war the service is more strictly carried on than in the Bastille. Now against whom do they make war?

[BST] Bournon: "Linguet, in this regard, exaggerated nothing....It would be possible to cite several examples of prisoners found dead in the morning in their cell." He agrees that the thick walls and heavy doors slowed any response. Bournon, 153.

[97]

The key is searched for: it is found. The Surgeon must then be called up: the Chaplain must also be roused, to complete the escort. All these people must necessarily dress themselves; so that, in about two hours, the whole party arrives with much bustle at the sick man's chamber.

They find him, perhaps weltering in his blood, and in a state of insensibility, as happened to me; or suffocated by an apoplexy, as ha happened to others. What steps they take, when he is irrevocably gone, I know not: if he still possesses some degree of respiration, or if he recovers it, they feel his pulse, desire him to have patience, tell him they will write next day to the Physician, and then wish him a good night

Now this Physician, without whose authority the Surgeon-Apothecary dare not so much as administer a pill, resides at the *Tuileries*, at three miles distance from the *Bastille*[BST]. He has other practice: he has a charge near the King's person; another near the Prince's. His duty often carries him to *Versailles:* his return must be waited. He comes at length: but he has a fixed annual stipend whether he do more or less; and, however honest, he must naturally be

---

[BST] At this time, the distinction between a physician (or medical doctor: *médecin*) and a surgeon (*chirugien*) went beyond a difference in specialization. Surgeons had long been confounded with barbers and had lost much of the prestige they had possessed in former centuries, but had begun to again demand and obtain recognition as skilled professionals. *Encyclopèdie*, Tome 3, 350-357. However, the surgeon-major in the Bastille still seems to have been on the older model, limited largely to bleeding and shaving prisoners. For some time, he also took on the apothecary's functions. He clearly had a subordinate relation to the physician, who was considered the best in Paris, but did indeed live some distance away. Notes for a new surgeon-major in 1750 say that he must live within the castle and inform castle personnel if he goes out, leaving word where he can be found. He must also have standard remedies – first aid – in his pharmacy. He was required to report on prisoners' illnesses and the remedies they required to the governor and other officials. He knew the prisoners not by their names, but by their residence: "The *calotte* of the *Bazinière* has split blood"; "The 3rd *Comté* had a stomach-ache all night." The turn-keys were also required to check if any prisoner had been sick overnight and to inform the surgeon if so. Bournon, 65-66, 153, 274, 289-291.

inclined to find the disorder as slight as may be, in order that his visits be the less required. They are the more induced to believe his representations, inasmuch as they are apt to suspect exaggeration in the prisoner's complaints: the negligence of his dress, the habitual weakness of his body, and the abjection no less habitual, of his mind prevent them from observing any alteration in his countenance, or in his pulse; both are always those of a sick man: thus he is oppressed with a triple affliction; first of his disorder; secondly, of seeing himself suspected of imposture, and of being an object of the raillery of the severity of the officers, for the monsters do not abstain from them even in this situation of their prisoner; thirdly, of being deprived of every kind of relief, till the disorder becomes so violent as to put his life in danger.

And even then, if they give any medicines, it is but an additional torment to him. The police of the prison must be strictly observed: every prisoner shut up by himself, by day and night, whether sick or in health, sees his Turn-key, as I have before observed, only three times a day. When a medicine is brought him, they set it on the table, and leave it there. It is his business to warm it, to prepare it, to take care of himself during its operation; happy, if the Cook has been so generous, as to violate the rules of the House, by reserving him a little broth; happy, if the Turn-key has been possessed of the humanity to bring it, and, the Governor to allow it. Such is the manner in which they treat the ordinary sick, or those who have strength enough to crawl from their bed to the fire-place[BST].

But when they are reduced to the last extremity, and to raise themselves from their worm-eaten couch, they are allowed a *guard*. Now let us see what this *guard* is. An invalid Soldier, stupid, clownish, brutal, incapable of attention or of

---

[BST] One man, says Madame de Staal, managed to see the surgeon – also the apothecary – twice a day (to enlist his help) on the pretext that he needed two enemas a day. The regent, informed of this, said, "Since they have only this to distract them, let's not deprive them of it." Staal, II, 433.

that tenderness so requisite in the case of a sick person. But what is still worse, this Soldier, when once attached to you, is never again permitted to leave you; but becomes himself a close prisoner. You must first, therefore, purchase his consent to shut himself up with you during your captivity; and if you recover, you must support, as well as you can, the ill-humour, discontent, reproaches, and vexation of this companion, who will be revenged on you in health for the pretended services he has rendered you in sickness[BST2]. Judge now of the insincerity of *D'Argenson*, the Lieutenant of Police, when he insisted on the temporal comforts prisoners experienced into the *Bastille*, and on the charity of the *Governors*.

Mass, confession and death

As to the spiritual, if these savages, equally incapable of shame and pity were at least susceptible of remorse, would they dare even to pronounce the word? What can it remind us of, but their outrages upon religion, for which they have no more respect, than they have for humanity?

First, let it be remarked, that every one is not permitted to go to Mass in the Bastille: this is a special favour granted only to a small number of elect. I confess, it was offered to me. The first day I was invited, they conducted me to a covered gallery, where I was to remain concealed, during the service: I did not, however, stay there long. Whatever slavery has of repugnance and horror, follows and oppresses you at the very foot of the altar[BST].

[BST2] More than once guards assigned to stay with prisoners had to leave because the conditions made them sick: "A certain Danry, invalid soldier, was put as company (so they call a guard placed with a prisoner) with the Count de Cagliostro. After staying 40 days, the boredom, the poor air of the apartment made him sick. He had to leave and was replaced." Danry, like others in that duty, was asked to get what information he could from the prisoner. *La Bastille dévoilée*, II, 68, cited in *Mémoires de Linguet*, 108-109.

[BST] The chapel was decorated with a painting of Saint Pierre-Aux-Liens (St. Peter-in-Chains), another example of the tactless decoration Linguet mentions in speaking of the clock. It was taken to the Hotel de Ville the day after the Bastille's fall. *Mémoires de Linguet*, 109.

They treat the Divinity at the Bastille much in the same manner as they do his likeness. The chapel is situated under a pigeon-house, belonging to the King's Lieutenant; it may be about seven or eight feet square[BST2]. On one of the sides they have constructed four little cages or niches, each to contain just one person: these have neither the enjoyment of light nor air, except when the door is open, which is only at the moment of entering, or going out. There do they shut up the unhappy votary. At the instant of receiving the sacrament they draw aside a little curtain, the covering of a grated window, through which, as through the tube of a spying-glass, he can see the person who performs this service. This mode of partaking in the ecclesiastical ceremonies appeared to me so shocking and disagreeable, that I did not a second time give way to the temptation of accepting their offer.

As to the *confession*, I know not how this matter is arranged: and I do not imagine that many of the captives, however devout, are desirous of having much to do with it. The Confessor is an officer of the higher order, on the establishment of the prison. Hence one may easily conceive with what security a prisoner might unbosom himself to this Confessor, supposing he had a conscience that wanted to be discharged[BST]. His office, then, is either a snare, or a mockery. It is beyond my conception, how they can have the audacity to propose to the prisoners in the Bastille, that they should open their souls to a base prevaricator, who prostitutes thus the dignity of his function; nor how a man, the hired instrument of the earthly power which oppresses them, can dare to address them in the name of Heaven that disavows him.

When a prisoner dies, whether after confession, or without it, I cannot say what they do with him; how they re-

---

[BST2] After Linguet's work appeared, the pigeon-house was removed. Bournon, 39-40.
[BST] Madame de Staal had similar qualms at first, but "Never was a suspicion less justified than that I had of our chaplain. I found in him the best man in the world, simple and compassionate, more disposed to pity my sorrows than to criticize my faults". Staal, 391.

venge themselves on the body for the flight of the soul, or where they suffer his allies to rest, when they are unable to torment them any longer[BST2]. Thus far I know, that they are not restored to his family. Surely, since the *first* establishment of the *Bastille,* some deaths must have happened in it: but who has ever seen a *mortuary extract* dated from it, except that of *Marshal Biron*[BST3]*?* Families are then abandoned without mercy to the confusion resulting from the absence of their head; and after the affliction they have suffered during his existence, they are denied even the said consolation they might derive from a certain knowledge of his fate.

Hope mocked

Readers, who have been but too much shocked at the barbarities I have already descanted on, you think yourselves, perhaps, arrived at the conclusion. It seems to you as if the imagination could not make a farther stretch in the art of devising torments beyond the multiplied refinements I have described. An assembly of executioners would reflect with indignation on the cool deliberation with which they were planned, and the calm indifference with which they are executed. Yet I think I can present you with something still more striking: I shall lay before you an anecdote that relates to me personally, and which exceeds all that you have hitherto heard.

From the 27th of September, 1780, to October, 1781, that is to say, during TWELVE MONTHS, I had not only remained in a total privation of all correspondence from without, or else in a correspondence worse than privation, as will be seen hereafter; but also in a no less absolute ignorance of all

---

[BST2] Deaths in the castle were duly recorded. Since the Bastille was in St. Paul's parish, Catholic prisoners were buried in St. Paul's cemetery. The Bastille paid the (modest) expenses. Bournon cautiously cites an account regarding a Bertin, who died in the Bastille March 3, 1779. That account says that his entry on the mortuary register was covered with a piece of paper, sealed with eight red wax seals marked "Royal Castle of the Bastille". Bournon, 154-155.

[BST3] Charles de Gontaut, Duc de Biron (1562-1602). A favorite of Henri IV, having plotted against him. he was sent to the Bastille and ultimately executed. *The Globe encyclopaedia of universal information,* 393-394.

transactions, whether of a public nature, or relative to my own affairs or, if they had suffered any intelligence to reach me, it was such only as was calculated to add to my despair, and to deprive me even of the consolation I might draw from the hopes of better treatment. Nay, many particulars, through a refinement in cruelty which sets all the powers of language at defiance, were false, fabricated purposely to lead me into error, and to render that error more afflicting, or more fatal.

Thus they told me repeatedly, with a sneer, that it was unnecessary for me to concern myself about what passed in the world, because I was there supposed to be dead; and they carried their deceit so far as to give me a detail of circumstances, which furious rage, or horrid wantonness had added to my pretended end. They assured me that I had nothing to expect from the zeal or fidelity of my friends; not so much because they were subjected to the same mistake with others concerning my death, as because they had *betrayed me*. This double imposture was intended not only to afflict me, but to inspire me with an unreserved confidence in the only traitor I had in reality to dread, whom they perpetually represented as the only faithful friend; and at the same time, to discover, by the manner in which I should receive these insinuations, whether I had in fact any secrets to expose me to treachery.

In October, 1781, the delivery of the Queen afforded me some glimmering of hope. This was a circumstance which they could not conceal from me: the discharge of the cannon over my head, and the public rejoicings before my eyes, proclaimed it. As these events always mark in France an epoch for the remission even of crimes, I conceived the idea, that this might extend the same bounty to innocence. I wrote a short letter to the Count *de Maurepas:* knowing his character, I strove to make it gay, nay almost merry. It seemed to have some effect on him; and to have disposed him to second the voice of the Public, which had at length declared itself in my favour. This alteration of his sentiments was not concealed from me: but, lest the circumstance should illude my mind with too consolatory reflections, they took care, at the same time, to inform me that he was dead; and that he died without having done any thing for me.

Denied a will

At length, in December 1781, my constitution giving way to so many trials and such variety of affliction; the physical and chymical operations, which for fifteen months had conspired with moral causes to undermine it, having now produced their effect; finding myself attacked in so brisk a manner, as not even to have the hope left, of being able to dispute the possession of my life any longer; perceiving every instant the approach of that in which I was about to lose not the light of day, for I could not discern it, but the sensation which rendered my existence the more excruciating torment, I began to think of making my WILL. For this an express permission was requisite. I petitioned for it, and begged the Ministers would allow me an interview with the public officer who alone could manifest my last intentions, that sole trustee, of whom I might acquire information indispensably necessary, in order not to make illusory dispensations.

On this subject I daily repeated, for the space of two months whilst my life was in danger, the most pressing, and, I may add, the most affecting intreaties. The Physician of the Bastille had the complaisance to carry in person to the Lieutenant of the Police, the Person acting immediately under the Ministry in affairs of this nature, a certificate of the state I was in, and of the imminent danger my life was exposed to. All the answer I obtained, was a merciless refusal: so that, after being fifteen months considered as dead, deprived of all the faculties of a living person, excepting only that of suffering, I lost the hope itself of enjoying, after I should really have ceased to breathe, the last rights, which no country denies to the deceased; to those, at least, who have not been degraded by a solemn justice.

It was thus I passed the entire months of December 1781, and of January 1782, fully persuaded every evening, that I should not see the dawn; and every morning, that I should not hear the conclusion of the day announced by that doleful clock, which, in this everlasting night, alone marks the divisions of time and, let it be remarked, that this expectation, though constantly deceived, became incessantly more painful, by means of that arbitrary caprice, which envied me even the satisfaction of leaving behind me testimonies of good-will, and marks of remembrance, to friends who might cherish and regret my memory.

I give the matter of fact; who will take it upon them to explain the motive?

They cannot object the regimen of the Prison, the pretended laws of that subverter of every law: for not only is not the rage of oppression carried to such excess, as make an alienation of all civil rights a rule that cannot be dispensed with, but it even sometimes imposes on its victims a necessity of discharging them. The Bastille has a warranted Notary. A prisoner then, in general, may exercise his civil functions: in the commencement of my captivity they not only permitted, but even obliged me to employ that Notary.

The *Exempt* of the Court of France, although seconded by the Plenipotentiary of the Police at Paris, having failed in his attempt to secure my papers at Brussels; and a third adjunct, detached to their assistance, not having at first met with better success, because there are laws, and those laws are respected in that country; they forced from me a letter of attorney, which served in part to accomplish their purpose. If, in order to pry into my secrets, to search for articles of accusation against me, or to enter into possession of my effects, they might, without infringing upon the Code of the *Bastille,* borrow the assistance of a public officer; surely it was neither more difficult, nor more dangerous, to permit me to call upon it, in order to dispose of what they had left me: a *Will* was no more illicit than a *Letter of Attorney.*

Had I even been accused, confronted, and had my process been instituted; yet, before judgment, a refusal of the power to make my will, and in consequence an anticipated confiscation, would be reckoned a most shameful and atrocious violation of justice: in what light then must it be considered, and how can it be qualified, situated as I really was, without judge, process, crime or accused? Was it not a most scandalous abuse of power, and a most convincing proof of the barbarous manner in which they sport with the life of the subject?

Types of prisoners

And let them not urge, I repeat it once more, that, the *Bastille* being exclusively destined for the confinement of *State Prisoners*, its regimen can neither be too severe, nor too mysterious; that, in consequence, the increase of rigour, which I find fault with, is only a further advance to its perfection, and to the true idea of the institution; since too much pains cannot be taken to convict or to disconcert dangerous persons whose freedom might bring about the subversion of their country.

But the fact is otherwise: the *Bastille* is not reserved, particularly of late, for the reception of State Prisoners alone. The facility with which it is opened is redoubled in proportion to the inhumanity with which its government is conducted. Within these few years it seems to have been the preliminary of the most ordinary civil offences the cognizance of which would appear to be the least susceptible, by their object and their issue, of this strange and terrible beginning. It is now in some measure become the anti chamber of the common jail.

A Woman of quality is suspected of having forged, or negotiated *false bills*: she is committed to the Bastille.

A madman, cloathed with the insignia of a Magistrate of Paris, accuses a woman who deals in hardwood at Lyons of having of having been the Treasurer of a society long since suppressed: she is committed to the *Bastille*. Released after this absurd story loses credit, she has a dispute, on account of some domestic concerns with a first clerk, who has some interest in her ruin: she is again committed to the *Bastille*.

A Deputy is charged with having been guilty of abuses in managing the affairs of an eminent House; but abuses which certainly did not affect the Government: they commit him to the *Bastille*.

Such was the lot of Lady *St. Vincent,* Mrs. *Roger,* and Mr. *Le Bel*[BST]. Were *they prisoners of State?* What then was the intention of subjecting them to this literary regimen?

All were removed before the ordinary Judges; but when they were removed, there was no proof whatever of their innocence. Far from that; one must conclude, that it appeared still more problematical, since they were delivered up to the tedious and expensive forms of justice, and to a deliberate and regular accusation. The discoveries then that were made previous to their remove, must have been rather adverse than favourable to them: since they incurred a less degree of suspicion when they entered, than when they quitted, that dangerous abyss; notwithstanding, it is on their entrance, that they are oppressed with the regimen of the prison! And they are not freed from it, until there is a strong presumption of

---

[BST] Mme. Saint Vincent claimed she had notes proving that Marshal Richelieu owed her one hundred thousand crowns. He denied it and had her sent to the Bastille for forgery. This became a lengthy and very public affair. In 1777, the Parlement decided the notes were forged, but not by whom. Her confrontation with Richelieu included the following exchange: "But Madame,' said the marshal, 'Please look at your person; Would anyone think it worth such an exorbitant sum?" —"I don't presume as much," she replied; "But you, Monsieur Marshal, look as well at your own, and you'll see that it would take at least that much to make it bearable."

At first poor, Madame Roger suddenly came into money, provoking suspicions that she was secretly helping the (then banned) Jesuits. She was sent to the Bastille, but quickly freed on the testimony of a M. Parent. However, several months later, Parent went bankrupt and demanded money she supposedly owed him. He now claimed she had been his mistress and that her sudden riches had come from her husband, who had been trying to hide part of his income. Among other things, Parent claimed that she had used her "attractive person" to seduce him. To which her lawyer replied that she could never have seduced a soul because "she looked like a grenadier disguised as a woman, and ... was terrifyingly ugly." (!)

Le Bel was privy to suspect activity by those in charge of the Count of Artois' finances. In order to silence him, they accused him of forgery and had him sent to the Bastille. This backfired when, to defend himself, he told everything he knew. Ultimately he was freed, but never completely exonerated, since Le Bel had been party to the acts in question. *Mémoires de Linguet,* 223-225.

their guilt! They are more than half restored in their liberty, when given up to a trial, which seems to threaten them with conviction; they were totally deprived of it, and all the severities of the prison were added to the privation, before even the preliminaries of the process were adjusted.

Further; the real *State Prisoners*, who arrive at the Bastille loaded with chains, which the pretext of the public good may justify, and pursued by a clamour which their crimes may excuse, find there uncommon indulgence, and a respect denied to all others.

Special treatment

I know not, for example, what misconduct had brought there, some time before me, a man who had been a clandestine agent, or in other words a spy, for the French marine[BST]. I am far from asserting that he merited his fate; but the accusation at least, on which the *Lettre-de-Cachet* was founded, must have been heavy indeed. He had been concerned in a very delicate business, the success of which did not correspond to his hopes, perhaps to his promises. The Minister who employed him, being accustomed by his old trade to consider secret intelligence as affording the finest field for a ministerial genius[17], and the most certain resource of government; thinking to manage the Marine Department like the Police, and flattering himself that he could lord it over the English fleet, in the same manner as he did over the entertainments of Paris, perhaps created this man his

---

[BST] Berville and Barrière say this was a Captain Montazeau, who'd plotted to seize a ship bound for America after he was refused its command. His good treatment was supposedly due to his wife's offering her favors to Sartines, then minister of the Navy. When Sartine learned that the wife, like her husband, had a venereal disease, he was furious, but yielded to her tears and finally freed her husband after six months in the Bastille. *Mémoires de Linguet*, 226-227.—When she came to visit her husband, De Launay himself stayed for the visit. She'd come with a little dog and spoke, supposedly to the dog, in Portuguese – a language her husband, but not De Launay, understood. This stratagem seemed successful. But the next time she came, the governor told her, "Madame, if your dog doesn't understand French, please avoid bringing him to the Bastille." *Ibid*, 122.

substitute in so perilious and degrading an office. Had he, as was imagined, in order to double, his profits, been guilty of a double treason, always to be apprehended from these sort of Agents? Commissioned by France to buy the secrets of England, had he sold to England those of France? Or did his Patron, misunderstanding his intelligence, or as was also affected, being urged by personal interest to neglect it, think, on seeing the consequences of his folly or his prevarication, that he must throw the blame on the shoulders of his Deputy, and feign to suspect his man's integrity, in order to cover his own incapacity, or something worse? I cannot say.

What I know is, that this man experienced, of the punishments of the Bastille, no one but the loss of liberty; that, from the very first moment, he was allowed books, and had permission to correspond with his friends: that while mine were justly alarmed by a silence no less calculated to deceive than to terrify, he was permitted to receive visits: that suspecting this, and being determined, in order to ascertain it, to incur the risk of mentioning it, in one of the rare and short interviews, with which I was favored by the Lieutenant of Police, who was well known to be a friend and creature of M. *De Sartines,* he acknowledged the fact, and imputed the extraordinary regard shown to the prisoner I named, to the *bounty* of the Minister, who was the author of his protection and on the observation I naturally suggested, that the mode of treatment should depend on the nature of the accusation, and not on the personal qualities of each Minister, he made this very remarkable answer: *That he could do me no otherwise than as he did, because there was no interest made for me*[BST].

[BST] Such use of influence could go quite far and was perfectly normal under the Old Regime (not only in regards to the Bastille). In 1761, a man was accused of trying to poison a banker whose wife he loved, and brought to the Bastille. But the wife was not arrested, and M. de Saint-Florentin (later de la Vrillière) wrote Sartines, "If you can avoid arresting the banker's wife, please do. You know that there are people here whom this concerns." *Mémoires historiques et authentiques sur la Bastille,* tome II, 292, cited in *Mémoires de Linguet,* 55n. Renneville says a criminal who was later to be sentenced to banishment "was fed deliciously, served the finest game, the tastiest fare, the most exquisite wines and was taken out every

So that the horrors of my captivity, the redundancy with which they heaped on me all the horrors of the Bastille, proceeded only from my misfortune in not being concerned in some dark and infamous intrigue; in not being sacrificed to a dextrous stroke of policy, which might conceal indulgence under the outward symptoms of severity; in having a Minister for a direct, personal, and implacable enemy, instead of an accomplice; in having no other protectors but men of worth; no other advocates but friends without influence; in short, in being committed by virtue of a *Lettre-de-Cachet* signed *Amelot*, and not *Sartines*.

Who would have conceived that, of those two Ministers, M. *De Sartines* should be the *man of benevolence*.

The regimen of the Bastille is then neither so inflexible, nor so uniform: but was it even uniformly rigid, it would not be the less detestable; since this rigour would be exercised equally on different offences; and, what is still more horrid, alike on innocence and guilt. But it is not possessed even of this abominable stability; and it deviates from it only in direct opposition to what justice would prescribe.

The above example; together with my own, prove that it will admit of some modification; that it is subordinate only to vengeance, or to the desire of the infernal monsters who direct it, to serve the resentment or the wants of their masters: they prove, that as the Ministry of France keep a good store of *Lettres-d-Cachet,* ready signed[18], which they wait only the moment of applying to use, for they likewise have in reserve a good quantity of tortures which they produce only when the fatal order is carried into effect; they prove that, there is in the Bastille a book of rates to regulate the tormenting, no less than the dieting of each prisoner; and that, in settling with the base suttler of Governor, who has the charge of subsisting them, the price of the provisions destined to prolong their existence; they determine also the measure of gall with which they are to be poisoned.

---

day to the terrace and the garden. Why? Because this criminal was one of D'Argenson's men." Savine, 82.

In the name of the King...

Is the regimen of the Bastille instituted then purposely to torment? and whom? Persons of acknowledged innocence; since very well-founded suspicions are productive either of indulgent treatment, or a removal. And in whose name? In the name of the King, of the supreme Magistrate, who is by his birth the protector of the innocent, the guardian of the feeble. It is by his intervention that these cruel effects are operated; it is by his immediate orders, that they declare themselves authorized to subject a wretch, who has given no offense either to him or to the laws, or to any thing which the laws require him to revere, to punishments unknown in the ordinary prisons, which are peopled with men either guilty; or, at least accused, of some of those offences! It is *on the part of the King* that they suffocate him in such a manner as not entirely to intercept respiration, but to leave him barely enough to prolong his agony; that they make a mockery of his sorrows; that they pride themselves on his misery; that they consider as so many triumphs the far fetched sighs forced out by his affliction: it is the King, whom they do not shudder to name as the author of those barbarous collusions which he is unacquainted with, of that ministerial vengeance which his heart disavows.

Yes, you are unacquainted with them; you, whom nature had given me for a Master, and whose virtues would have given me for a protector if your throne were accessible to innocence, as it is to calumny; you, whose esteem would be the most flattering recompense, and the most powerful encouragement of my labours; you, whose frank and ingenuous soul is equally incapable of any sentiment of fear at my promise of always declaring the truth, or of disgust at my exactness in fulfilling it.

You are entirely unacquainted with dungeons, which, nevertheless, are opened and thus only in your name; in which existence is only measured by suffering, and from which even hope itself is oftentimes excluded; which daily swallow up citizens of irreproachable character, faithful and zealous subjects, who in vain from the bottom of those dreary abodes call on the name and virtues of their Prince; that sacred name, which in every other place is the surety for the execution, but here serves merely to authorize the infringement of the laws.

In signing a warrant for imprisonment, you think yourself only making a legitimate use of your authority, consecrated by the possession of several ages; an use necessary to the public repose, and from which no abuses take their origin: you suppose that the execution of this order is attended only with the precautions necessary to secure it.

Beneficent even in the rigours which your high office compels you to authorize, you have given a thousand proofs of your inclination to alleviate evils which the preservation of society requires. By your ordination, the prisons destined to ensure the conviction and the chastisement of vice, are becoming more tolerable and less oppressive; they are no longer a preliminary punishment, often more cruel than the final sentence. You have overturned the savage practice by which the Courts of Justice were authorized to put persons accused, or only suspected, to the torture, in order to try if only be those means they could not render them criminal[19]. You are far from suspecting, that in your kingdom, in your capital under your eyes, there exists a place specially devoted to perpetuate on innocence a *question* infinitely more cruel that all the *preparatory questions* you have proscribed; for these latter racked only the body; whereas those of the Bastille torment the body the more effectually to distract the mind. You are far from suspecting that they make arbitrary additions of their own to this infernal regimen; that the subaltern agents, appointed to maintain it, find both satisfaction and profit in abusing it; that like those ravenous dogs, who tear and bite the game in fetching it, they take pleasure in barbarity, when all that is required in them is fidelity and obedience.

But you shall continue no longer in this ignorance. Direct your eyes to those subterranean sepulchers, which the light has never enlivened with its presence. To enable me to point them out to you, two events were requisite, the one no less singular than the other; that I should enter them, and find my way out again. The second, which, I owe to you alone, assures me that the knowledge, for which I am indebted to the first, will not be unattended with advantage.

It will indeed cost me my Country. The necessity of seeking for a tomb among strangers, alas! among enemies, will be the sole reward of all the sacrifices I have made to her. This is the last and I shall be repaid for all the others, if this last should not be fruitless.

But it cannot be so; your heart is touched with sensibility; you shew marks of commiseration, of indignation: those emotions surely cannot arise in vain. Endued with all the power of a God to protect your subjects, and honoured with all his attributes, when you exert it, give to Europe, give to the world the sight of a miracle, which you are worthy to perform. Speak the word; at the sound of your voice, we shall behold the downfall of that modern Jericho, a thousand times more deserving than the ancient of the thunder of heaven, and the curse of men. The reward of this noble effort will be an accumulation of glory, an increase of the affection of your people for your person and family, and the universal benefaction, not only of the present, but of every age to the remotest posterity.

NOTES.

(1) *Page* 28 — In placing the tower of London as a parallel to the Bastille, it would be unjust, and even criminal, not to remark, that between these two prisons there is more intrinsic difference than outward resemblance. The Governors of the Tower, and the garrison employed to execute their orders, are subject to the authority of the Parliament, like other subjects. A prisoner, finding himself ill treated by them, has a thousand means of carrying his complaints to the superior powers, or to his friends and relations, who are interested in supporting them. There the prisoner is *certain of a fair and public trial.* He has Attorney, Council; every thing, which he must endeavour to prove, or to confute, is communicated to him in the most ample manner. The accusation of an repeatable offence against the State, marks only the prison to which he is to be consigned, but makes no alteration whatever in the process by which his fate is to be decided. Finally, in the very delays and severities that may accompany it, there is never the least shadow of doubt, not only concerning his existence; but even with regard to the state of his health, or the place of his confinement. Is that the *Bastille?*

(2) *Page* 54—Here perhaps some caviller, or some member of Administration, may charge me with Hyperbole: perhaps they may pretend to affirm, that there are few countries where there is not a prison equivalent to the Bastille, in which the conditions may be more shocking, and the abuses more flagrant. By such a comparison may they attempt to justify, in an indirect manner, that abominable regimen, which every honest mind must revolt at, and which the most steady partisans could never defend but by similar subterfuge.

But let us deprive them of this resource. I allow that in almost every country the *good of the public* has frequently operated as a motive to justify the exercise of extraordinary rigour, but it is not true that, in any country, the laws or even immemorial custom, have consecrated any thing to be put in competition with the regimen of the Bastille. Whatever repugnance I may feel in handling this disagreeable subject, with whatever disgust the idea of prolonging the consideration of it may inspire me, let us search the annals of tyranny; let us over-run the globe, and seek, in the history of the enormities of arbitrary power, for a parallel to the institution of the Castle which hangs, a disgraceful monument, over the street of St. Anthony in Paris.

This short retrospect of past or foreign miseries will perhaps make more impression than the most energetic description of our own. By seeing what have been in every age the fruits of these *Lettres-de-cachet*, and by comparing them with those which they still produce, our modern *Tituses*[20], may the more easily decide, whether it will not be most conducive to their interests, to make use of an engine of this kind, and to rival the ingenuity of a *Phalaris*, or a *Nero*.

I repeat it, then, once more, and am ready to prove it, that in the whole universe there has never been any thing similar to the *regimen of* the *Bastille*. We have ever heard of a nation reduced to so abject and ignominious a servitude as to have a *Bastille* constantly in existence; a gulf incessantly open for the reception of men; not, let it be remarked, to punish, but to torment them; a political purgatory, where the most trifling misdemeanors, nay innocence itself, are often arbitrarily doomed to the pains of Hell.

In antiquity you will not find a *Prison of State*, excepting such as were used by certain abominable tyrants, and that only during their own reign. They were like the sword and the pestilence, transitory scourges; which were used only during the usurpation of those execrable oppressors, and which perished with them: they were not inseparably attached to the constitution of the country; they were not one of the favorite springs of government, or the habitual engine of authority. What we can learn of their Police will not permit us, in any sense, to liken them to the Bastille.

We read, for instance, that Dionysius the Elder had one in

his palace at Syracuse[21]: he had even, as history informs us, practiced a refinement, which, we have cause to wonder, has not been adopted by some of the subaltern tyrants, who have followed his steps with so much success in bringing to perfection the regimen of the Bastille. The vaults of the dungeons were emulated with such art, that every thing which, was uttered resounded, and was heard distinctly in a closet, that served as a receptacle for these accumulated sounds. This was the observatory, or, if you will have it, the confession-box, where the Tyrant took post to intercept the secret conversation of the prisoners: and this curious cabinet was called the EAR.

Nevertheless this EAR could not have been always faithful in its report: for they relate that a Philosopher having been committed there by *Lettre-de-cachet*[22], and afterward released, the Tyrant asked him, how the prisoners employed their time in it? "In wishing for thy death," replied his captive, with more sincerity than discretion. That was a secret then, which the EAR had not revealed, and of which the consequence was, if we are still to believe the story, *another Lettre-de-cachet,* ordering the execution of all the prisoners.

But however it may be with this latter circumstance, as the EAR was constructed to betray the conversation of the prisoners, it follows, that they were allowed to converse; that they had an intercourse with each other: they were not abandoned to total solitude: it was not, then, as it is in the Bastille.

Among the Romans there was neither EAR, nor BASTILLE. In the time of the Republic a Citizen, though guilty, could not be arrested till after his condemnation; and this was usually prevented by a voluntary exile: still less reason, therefore, had, innocence to dread these arbitrary dungeons.

Under the Emperors, Rome was not exempt from assassinations, sanctified by the authority of the sovereign power: but these sacrifices were made in the houses of the victims. The *Lettre-de-cachet* countersigned *Sejanus, Narcissus, Tigellinus*[23], *&c.* which commanded the execution, was notified by a Tribune, or a Centurion at the head of a party of Soldiers. The military in every part of the world, like the dogs who tear and devour the game, are the persons charged with this honorable office.

At sight of the Ministerial Mandate, some took poison; others had recourse to the poignard; and others again caused their veins to be opened. The Soldiers surrounded the house until the business was over; and then went quietly to their barracks, as if they had come from mounting a guard.

Some persons will not fail to exclaim that this is worse still than the Bastille. I cannot pretend to say it is not; but think it a question, which those who have been there, are best qualified to decide. If I were to judge by my own feelings; the summary and expeditious method of the Romans would appear to me by far the most eligible. I implored a thousand times, both verbally and in writing, either a trial, or death; the bath of Seneca, or the poignard of Thraseas, I should at that time have considered a favour[24].

But without pronouncing a positive judgement on this subject, it is at least certain, that they did not envy those whose existence they were anxious to exterminate, the consolation of *making their will*, before they should quit it. On the contrary this was the recompence of a prompt obedience: the privilege of making their last arrangements, and the certainty of their being carried into execution, were, according to *Tacitus*[25], the *pretium sestinandi*[26]. But we have seen how, in the Bastille, the same resignation, the approach of a death which I hastened by my vows, did not afford me the same indemnity. There is, therefore, on the one side, an advantage, not to be found on the other: at Rome, in these cases, death was the more certain; in France, they contrive to render its approaches the more painful.

But that is not all; this murderous precipitation was fatal only to the Great; and the monsters who had required it, rarely escaped the weight of public vengeance. Sejanus was torn to pieces by the populace[27]; Nero, proscribed by a solemn decree, had fallen a victim to an ignominious death, if he had not anticipated it, by laying violent hands upon himself: moreover, at times, Trajans and Antonines[28] arose to deliver Rome from this opprobrious practice, and to interrupt the course of what would otherwise have been at length considered as one of the just prerogatives of the Sceptre.

Under the worst Princes we find that those *guilty,* or rather *accused* of *offences against the State,* were subjected only to a disagreeable constraint; not to a horrid captivity. They fastened one of their hands to that of a Soldier, and thus prevented them from quitting one another. Such an association certainly could not be very agreeable; but it neither hindered Agrippa[29] from keeping quietly in his own house under Tiberius, nor St. Paul from preaching publickly under Nero. Was that the confinement of a Bastille?

The only Species of *State Prison,* constantly kept up in antient Rome, was what was called the *Transportation*[30]. There were certain little islands, which they peopled with persons suspected by the Court. From these they were forbid to emigrate, on pain of death. I confess, that such warrants cannot on any principle be justified; yet still the unfortunate persons, thus disfranchised, were allowed the enjoyments of light and air; they were allowed a part of their income; they were permitted to take some of their servants along with them; they corresponded with their friends: in fine, if they became so weary of their situation, as to prefer a total dereliction of their country, they had it in their power to escape and they frequently did so. One may perceive, that this still falls short of the Bastille.

The history of the LOWER EMPIRE being far from exact, it is impossible to trace in detail the use made of *Lettres-de-cachet*. The pretended Emperors being made and unmade with as little ceremony as the Deys of Algiers, their Ministers had scarcely the time requisite to render the prisons of state subservient to their vengeance. Instead of mewing up the subject, they cut his throat at once: and this policy was often adopted by those whose reign was esteemed, brilliant and happy.

Constantine had a method peculiar to himself: he caused those whom he wished to get rid of without noise or scandal, such as his wife, his son, &c. to be suffocated in warm baths[31]: his father-in-law he strangled, and his brother-in-law he beheaded. The Bishops were the only persons he seemed to spare; and them he was content to banish: but it does not appear that he imprisoned any.

One would be apt to suspect, that, under his son Constantius, they began to lay the foundations of a *Bastille:* for some troubles having arisen in a Council held by his order; the Fathers having been divided, and matters carried to some violence, the Provincial Governors, whose business it was to execute the *Lettres-de-cachet,* imprisoned several; and one of them, named Lucifer, wrote to the Emperor in the following terms[32]:

"Because we retired from your iniquitous Council, we languish in prison, deprived of the light of the Sun; kept close in darkness, and without being permitted to receive visits from any one." That is indeed the picture of a *Bastille.*

Yet, on the one hand, we must remark, that the Prelate had permission to address himself directly to the Sovereign, and to complain to him of the rigours of his confinement; which is a point precisely forbidden by the *Bastillian Code;* and on the other, that it is probable, if so admirable an invention had been once introduced into the Empire, it would have been perpetuated there, and that it would not have been necessary to look forward to the time of Louis XI for its resurrection: now no traces of it whatever remain in Constantinople. When they wished to get rid of St. Chrysostom, they sent him to Caucasus; instead of decoying him by the immobility of a dungeon, they caused him to perish by a violent journey[33]; they did not even conceive the idea of shutting him up in a fortress, where he would be thought dead while yet in existence.

In the Greek empire, the Secretaries of State and their deputies soon discovered the advantage of depriving of the light those persons, whom they thought at the same time deserving of their attention and their resentment: but they never thought of these caves, hollowed in walls twenty or thirty feet thick: they made directly to the eyes themselves, instead of striving to render them useless; they tore them out, or burnt them with rods or plates of heated metal sometimes, they scalded them with boiling vinegar: and all by virtue of a *Lettre-de-Cachet.*

These *State Criminals* were blinded, I confess: but the

despotic mandate, by which they were devoted to such martyrdom, was not founded on the *Laws of the State:* there was no Minister particularly appointed to the department of *blinding.* The *Lieutenant of the Police* of *Constaninople* was not, by an express brevet, created Imperial Commissary for the application of boiling vinegar, or for administering these burning patents.

In modern Constantinople, that scandal of our pretended philosophy, and of our boasted humanity there is a fortress, which seems to bear some affinity to the Bastille. I mean the Prison of the *Seven Towers*[34], which our travellers call a *State Prison;* but which, by their very relations, we may perceive, is rather a magazine than a prison. They seldom confine in it any but the Ambassadors of the Christian Powers, who break with them; and there they not only see whom they please, but are even served by their own domestics.

Slaves, whose ransoms are stipulated, but not paid, are sometimes obliged to await there the completion of the bargain: and it is then no less an *asylum* to them, than a *security* to their Masters. Living at their ease, well fed, and often visited, it is rather an anticipation of liberty which they *enjoy,* than a captivity which they *suffer*[35].

But they have never yet thought of shutting up in that prison, purposely to languish there, and to undergo a sequestration more rigorous than that of the most atrocious offenders, men, to whom no crime has been imputed. Never did Sultan, Visir, Cady, or Jannissary, take into his head to give, to solicit, or to execute a *Lettre-de-cachet,* against a Citizen of Constantinople, of Erzerum, or Salonica, for having found the aigrette of the *Grand Visir* less brilliant than usual, or the robe of the *Selictar* ill-embroidered[36].

If a man is so daring, as to blaspheme against the PROPHET, he is circumcised or impaled: the law is precisely defined, and he has the alternative before him. If a visir makes an ill use of his power, he is banished, and stripped of his possessions; sometimes he is strangled. But why would he be made Visir? why was he avaricious? If a baker uses false weights, and thus robs the public, he is punished as a robber; the punishment prompt, and often terrible: but the crime and conviction always precede it. All the inhabitants of that vast Empire[37], Greeks, Armenians, Franks, Asiatic, Europeans, Tartars, Catholics, Schismatic, Cophtis, Jews, Mussulmans, &c. pass their days in perfect ease and security, if they only conform to the laws; and, above all, if they have the happiness to be unknown in the Seraglio: they have not even the idea of *Bastille,* or a *Lettre-de-cachet.*

In Persia, during the time of her glory and prosperity, that is to say, till the civil wars, by which she has within half a century been depopulated[38], these sources of Ministerial vengeance not only were equally unknown; but the ordinary justice had found means to spare persons accused, and even presumed guilty, the humiliation and horror of a dungeon. Their prisons were moveable. The man whom it was necessary for the preservation of the public tranquillity to secure, lost no more of his liberty than was requisite to prevent his withdrawing himself from punishment, and from committing any new offences. With an ingenuity that partook more of compassion than severity, they had invented a kind of portable wooden triangle, called the *Cango*[39]; which, fixed round his neck, and inclosing one of his hands, could neither be concealed, nor taken off; and yet did not prevent him from discharging his ordinary functions. Carrying about with him, thus, a guard of little expence, he still retained the enjoyment of light and life; the power of regulating his affairs, and the means of vindicating his innocence; without ceasing to be in the hands of the civil power charged with the verification of it. We are told of bloody executions ordered, or perpetrated, by drunken Monarchs: but these horrors were confined to the *Harems;* and the institution alone of the *Cango* proves, that the general spirit of the nation, without excepting that of the Government, was tempered no less with mildness than equity. It is the same in the Empire of the Mogul, in India, China, and Japan. In this last country, from which our own restlessness has justly expelled us[40], we are assured, by the relations of those who have visited it that the manners are savage, and the punishments equally prompt and cruel. It may be so but, at any rate, the celerity will compensate for the barbarity of an execution. They are there ignorant of those long detentions which eternize the most horrid of all torments the despair produced by the uncertainty of the term to one's miseries.

The man whom they embowel, whom they precipitate on tenter-hooks, whom they cut in ten thousand pieces, whom they pound alive in a mortar; if it be true, that those exquisite tortures art common; this man, I say, has been tried; he has had an opportunity of defence, of justification: it is by the Magistrate, by the Laws, and not by caprice, that he is devoted.

Our missionaries have often been inhabitants of the Indian prisons. Strangers, unknown, preaching novelties, which must have appeared singular even to those who weighed and considered them with the most composure, but which must have appeared dangerous and criminal to the Magistrates, and above all to the Priests, whose professed enemies they declared themselves, there could be none against whom severity would be more lawful, or *Lettres-de-cachet* more excusable; not withstanding, they have been obliged to do justice to the humanity of the Judges who detained them, of the Jailors who looked after them, of the People of the country, who visited, comforted and fed them.

We see among them no examples similar to those of our Royal Castles, and the warrants by which they are filled; if we except what is related of the Princes of the Blood, baptized by the Jesuits; who were, first exiled, and afterwards imprisoned by the Emperor Jontching[41]. The Missionaries, who report their catastrophe, have not informed us of the cause but whatever it might have been their relation proves, that there was no *Bastille* in China, since they were obliged to build one on purpose for each of the Princes destined to suffer that imprisonment.

And, even then, it was not a clandestine apprehension, effected in private by *Exempts of the Police*, which left equally in a state of ambiguity, the life of the prisoners. their crime or their innocence. These momenteous prisons were openly constructed; and it was not neglected to render them conspicuous, as the signal punishments of an atrocious offence. which doubtless must have been known by the people of the country.

But in the midst of all this dreadful rigour, the sufferers still met with some alleviation: they sometimes were permitted to be attended by their domestics: they received spiritual succour from the authors of their misfortune: the communication was open for intelligence from their families; they were supplied from their own houses with meat, drink, and clothes; in short with all that is scrupulously excluded from the Bastille.

In all Asia, we cannot find a regular *State Prison,* established on the fundamental principles of Government, except in Ceylan. "There," says a traveler, "the King has a number of prisoners, who are chained, some in the ordinary prisons, others in custody of the Nobles. No one dares to enquire their offence, or the time they have been confined: they are kept thus for five or five years and whenever they are imprisoned, it is by the King's order."

This is indeed somewhat like the Bastille: the State Mysteries of *Ceylan* resemble a little those of the Street *St. Antoine* But observe that we hear nothing of dungeons specially appointed to swallow up those wretches, whose crimes and whose catastrophe are so imperiously consigned to silence and darkness: they are either shut up in the *ordinary prisons,* or entrusted to the *custody* of *the Nobles.*

In the first case, they experience only all evil common to all accused persons. In the second, they should find in these private, though *Royal* jails every kind of consolation. One cannot imagine, that a Nobleman of *Candi* or *Columbo* would assume the disposition because required by a despot for a time to discharge the duty of a Governor of the *Bastille.* It is besides evident, that none of these tawney Gentlemen could have in their houses, those windows and chimneys interlaced with iron bars; those walls of thirty feet thickness; nor those closets, which are prisons within a prison, and which cause a variety of misery, no less painful than ignominious.

All, then, is clearly exempt from a pestilence, which among us destroys such a number of Citizens.

In America there are many other kinds of oppression; and in Africa likewise: but they know nothing of this. The Indians in the new world are trampled on by merciless tyrants, who are themselves debased by superstition; part of the African coast is subject to an arbitrary government, which has the evils and abuses alone of that which prevails in Asia. The remainder owes its miseries but to our commerce: it is the Merchants of Europe who carry out chains for the inhabitants of Congo, or of Juida[42], and not their Princes who forget them: they are sold, they are devoted to a life of labour: but no Minister has a right to condemn them for his own pleasure, to a destructive inactivity. They certainly lead a wretched life at the *Antilles:* but it is a wretchedness of another kind, and one that admits, of much alleviation and solace. They have have their wives, their children: their exactness in the discharge of their duty may save them from the rod of the *Overseers:* but it can save no one from a *Lettre-de-cachet,* and from the discipline that follows.

Is it in Europe then alone that there dreadful scourges are to be dreaded? and in what parts of Europe are we to dread them? We know it is not in Great-Britain. An arbitrary detention would there be treason against *the People;* which would be punished with no less rigour than treason against *the King:* and I have already done homage to that well-known fact, that even in those detentions, which may be authorised by a higher interest and by motives of public good, the person accused, the prisoner, nay the guilty, are deprived of none of the rights or resources of innocence.

In Germany, the Princes are in general pretty despotic, in the usual acceptation of the word; that is to say, there is no barrier to obstruct the exertion or abuse of their authority: notwithstanding, they have no *Bastille,* nor any equivalent. There is nothing to prevent them from indulging in this amusement: but, whether the idea be peculiar to the Ministry of large States; whether the recourse that might be had to the Emperor, or to the Tribunals that actually exist, and the fear of giving too much influence to these objects of their jealousy, who would not fail to take the advantage of it, restrain the Proprietors of the Grand Fiefs; or whether the people, of a docile and patient disposition, neither enlightened much by knowledge nor enslaved by their passions, are obedient enough without being subjected to this yoke, I do not perceive, from the *Rhine* to the *Oder*, the shadow of a *Bastille* excepting *Spandaw*.

But, first, *Spandaw* belongs to a Monarchy purely military. This colossus, which took its rise in our days, and by force attained an elevation no less astonishing than rapid, should preserve in its constitution, something of its original. Secondly, it is for the Soldiery, that the *Bastille* of *Brandenbourg* is specially destined. This unlucky honour is but rarely conferred upon the Citizens and as to Soldiers, who know no other interpreters but the bayonet and the cannon, what right have they to complain, if sometimes addressed by a *Lettre-de-cachet?*

In Denmark, I do not find that Kings, or their Ministers, have been tempted to let off any, since the times of the abominable Christiern[43]; nor that Jutland or Famia have groaned under so useless, or so destructive a mass of building as a *Bastille*. In Sweden no Sovereign has sullied his reign either by building, or making use of them.

Lastly, in Russia, where, of all the countries in the world, their ancient manners would seem to be the most compatible with a *Bastille* and its appurtenances, a contrary system has been adopted. *Lettres-de-cachet* are there indeed in all their vigour; but the consequences are extremely different: a province is there become a *Prison of State*. In France, the confined dimensions of his prison is one of the most afflicting torments to a prisoner; in Siberia they lament the immensity of theirs. The former are buried in real sepulchers; the latter are lost in unbounded deserts. However miserable these last may be, it is evident that they are the least to be lamented. They have some indemnification and amusement. Their families accompany them, or follow them; if their hearts are often distracted on thinking what they have lost, they may comfort themselves by making the most of what remains: they at least grieve together; and the only bitter tears are those which are shed in solitude.

Besides, the activity of the life which they are obliged to lead, preserves them from weariness, from the torment of reflecting always on the past, and of trembling at the idea of the future. They are doubtless, very miserable; but they would

[125]

think themselves much less so if they were acquainted with *French Siberia*.

In Spain, I believe there are two or three Towers used by the Ministry as springs of government, and necessary engines of the State: yet have they been hitherto but thinly peopled, on account of their rival prisons of the Inquisition. A people who bear this latter yoke, and bear it peaceably, cannot be brought into question in regard to the former.

In Italy, as in Germany, this last is little known. Nevertheless, there exist, at Rome, and at Venice, undoubted marks of arbitrary power; in the one a castle, and in the other a tribunal, both of which are equally scandals to justice, and arms, ever ready for the grasp of despotism. Yet the multitude of strangers, who are perpetually visiting those celebrated cities proves that the use is not so frequent, as the outward shew is dreadful. When an Englishman or a Hamburger embark for Rome, to hear oratorios, and gaze at St. Peter's, or to dance at a masquerade in Venice, their friends do not anxiously conjure them to beware of the *Castle of Adrian*[44], or of the *Inquisition of State*. But there is no stranger going to France, who is not cautioned to beware of the *Bastille*. Thus, both according to fact and opinion, the Bastille stands alone, an unrivalled monument.

(3) *Page* 63.–I do not here pretend to reflect on the operations of Mr. Necker. I have indeed had much reason to complain of him; and also of his Wife, who was still more of a Minister than he was; but these private prejudices should not influence the judgment of an impartial writer, when he adverts to the public conduct of a man entrusted with power. Mr. Necker has still very numerous partisans: he introduced in France a glimmering hope, and there must have been no small merit in that, of a restoration of the public credit. If he had not been counteracted by a ruinous war, or rather by the weak and expensive prodigality with which the naval affairs of the kingdom were conducted, his operations might have been productive of some advantage lo his country.

(4) *Page* 68.–They soon granted me permission to write. This may seem to have been a very striking mark of

benevolence, and a prodigious consolation: yet who could imagine, what notwithstanding is but too true, that this grant was an additional vexation to me?

1°. The paper, of which an account was kept, was given me by rule, and a receipt taken; with this reservation, that I could never get a fresh supply, without accounting for the method in which I employed the old one; a species of slavery, which no one can estimate without having experienced it.[BST]

2°. It may be easily conceived, that I should not be tempted to apply this paper to any other use, but that of writing letters, or memorials, relative to my release. Now to whom was I to address them? To the Ministers? From them I could get no answer and my situation proves, that it was not to them I was to look up for relief! To my friends or patrons? I was aware that nothing passed, that nothing ever would find its way to them. I was informed that *they thought me dead;* and that those who could not be so mistaken, shewed no other sentiment but that of indifference. At the end of about eight months, they allowed me the correspondence of the *Sieur Le Quesne**, whose zeal and probity they were continually crying up to me.

(5) *Page* 83. They have a double reason for it. First, as the only intermediate persons, who have a commerce with the prisoners, they are necessarily their confidants, and receive their complaints, nay sometimes may be subject to their ill-humour. Ill paid and contemptuously treated by their superiors, they expect some gratification from such prisoners as despotism has not devoted to a perpetual captivity: uncertain whether it will lead to a scaffold, or to a place at

---

[BST] Other prisoners tell similar tales. Dumouriez at one point wrote with a buckle, though he says Sartines let him take his notes with him when he left. He later had enough writing materials to leave some hidden away in columns in one of his rooms, for the use of future prisoners. II, 268, 289, 299. Many found ways around the limits on paper, using paper that had wrapped chocolate, drugs, etc., writing on blank pages of books and even – as one official wearily notes - writing notes on plates to communicate with each other. Du Noyer, 156; Savine, 143, 149; Bournon, 269.

* See the Introduction, P. i [*Original translator's note* This reference, from the original editor, makes no obvious sense - JC]

Court, whether it will terminate in a legal assassination, like *Lally,* or in a marshal's staff, like *Belle-Isle*[BST], and so many others, they sometimes condescend to shew a little commiseration.

Humanity may also sometimes act upon rustic hearts, not yet hardened by opulence: I owe this justice to that rank of men in the Bastille to declare, that they are the only persons endowed with it. The common soldiers are there, as every where else, stupid machines, directed by the rod, and know nothing out of their own kennel. The officers of the higher *Etat Major* join to this bare servility the insolence and severity inspired by habitual command: the *Etat Major* of Turn-keys, the medium between the *two, is* the only rank susceptible of pity.

But they have another good reason for opposing the retrenchments of the table, which the niggardly disposition of the Governor promotes, or at least for wishing him a little more generous; which is, that the remains are their property: and it is difficult to conceive how jealous Mr. *De Launay* is of this circumstance. If he and his Minister can but preserve their places a little longer. I doubt not, but a letter will come, signed *Amelot*, which will put a stop to so dreadful a disorder.

But if these important trustees of State secrets had not also little secrets of their own; if the silence which covers their barbarity towards the prisoners, was not equally necessary to conceal the shameful iniquity of their private conventions with one another; it would be easy, for the Governor to assign his motives for the avarice which now presides over the victualling of his tavern.

He considers as his own patrimonial estate, the sixty thousand livres a year attached to his appointment; and with reason: for he has purchased it, and that dearly enough.

He obtained the *survivorship* in the time of the Count de

[BST] Charles Louis-Auguste-Fouquet, Count de Belle-Isle (1684-1761) was the grandson of the disgraced superintendent Fouquet, but steadily progressed in his military career until becoming a Marshal of France. He was briefly in the Bastille. *Biographie universelle*, Tome III, 565-567.

Jumilhac^{BST}, but this gentleman exacted, as a condition of his accepting a co-adjutor, the sum of an hundred thousand crowns, which were paid to him and his son's marriage with Mr. De Launay's daughter, thought a rich heiress; which took place accordingly.

But not withstanding this compact, Mr. De Launay, being a man neither of family, nor connexions, having neither services to plead, nor interest to recommend him might have met with a refusal, if he had not been so fortunate as to have a brother in the service of the Prince of Conti[45]. This brother prevailed on the Prince to make interest with the Minister, whose clerks expedited their patents signed *Amelot*; and to recompense the zeal of the younger, the happy elder brother secured him a pension of ten thousand livres a year on the revenues of his place.

This bargain is well known in the Bastille; there is not a scullion but is informed of it. But why should it afford matter for scandal? Every officer there lies under the same predicament. The employment of *King's Lieutenant* is worth about 8000 livres per annum: the present possessor gave his predecessor a sum of money; the amount I know not: but I know, that he besides gives him a pension of a thousand crowns per annum[BST].

Those of the turn-keys are worth about 900 livres a year. They are usually filled up from some of the Governor's old domestics; thus are they made executioners, as a reward for length of service: but this reward itself is not gratuitous; for there is not one, who is not obliged either to pay a premium

---

[BST] Antoine-Joseph-Marie Jumilhac de Cubjac. Governor from May 29, 1761 to October 1776. The governor before De Launay. Dumouriez describes him as "an old man in a dressing gown... Never did man have a character less matched to his awful job; he had accepted it because it kept him in Paris with 60,000 pounds of income.; ...he was good, sensitive and polite." Dumouriez, II, 260. Bournon confirms Linguet's account of the conditions of De Launay's installation. Bournon, 94.

[BST] Bournon says that Linguet was wrong. Charges in the Bastille were not venal. Any arrangement would have been between the two men. Bournon, 57.

on accepting the office, or an annual stipend to some person or other[BST2].

In fine, the department of *washing* itself is not exempted from this maxim of frittering and sub-dividing. The titular washerwoman receives from the King about three halfpence a shirt; she performs the business by deputy, who leaves her a third part, and does up the linen for a penny. Thus it is, that the *service of the King,* and that of the *prisoners,* is performed: such is the brokerage, to which they prostitute these *offices of trust.* To such hands is the life of an innocent man committed, who can only be reproached with a misfortune much oftener attached to virtue than to vice, of having numerous and powerful enemies.

(6) *Page* 86. It is well known, that the crimes of the notorious *Brinvilliers*[46], in the last century, originated from the education which her lover had received in the *Bastille.* An Italian named *Exili,* whom they had appointed the partner of his cell, was his preceptor. This proves, by the way, no less than the memoirs already referred to, that in those times they were unacquainted with the solitude and privations of every kind, which at present form its characteristic principle: yet it certainly was not the danger of a similar tuition that has brought about the modern reform.

But we have nothing to say at present to the fatal theory of *Exili;* I only allude to the facility of imitating the practice. Now this certainty subsists in the *Bastille,* in proportion to the impotence of a prisoner to guard against it, should the government be disposed to get rid of him in that manner; and to the impotence no less absolute, I do not say of coming at any proof of the crime, supposing the fatal deed perpetrated in consequence of insinuations from some other quarter, but even to collect the most distant token of it. If, in this second case, Government cannot be directly reproached with the crime, yet still must it be considered as an accomplice, from the facility it affords for the perpetration. A traveler is set

---

[BST2] Bournon says that the turn-keys were in fact carefully chosen, trusted men: "Linguet was wrong, once more, to say… they were chosen among old lackeys of the governor." They were "*à la nomination du Roi*", that is, in theory, named by the King. Bournon, 72.

upon by two ruffians in a wood: could he, who only held the unfortunate man's arms, whilst the other cut his throat, plead that he was not a confederate in the murder?

Virtuous and benevolent Princes, is not this idea sufficient to inspire you with horror? By the regimen of the Bastille your name is daily liable to become an instrument of the basest of crimes, and, at the same time, an impenetrable veil to cover it. You would punish the man who had the audacity to propose, that you should serve out with your own sacred hands a beverage mortal to the victims of Ministerial tyranny; and yet, by this infernal regimen, the *Lettre-de-cachet*, which they force from you, assures these very Ministers the means of pouring it out themselves with impunity.

The Jailors, whom they employ, will exclaim, that the mere suspicion is an insult to their feelings! But again, are the laws which expressly prohibit *private imprisonment*[47], which ordain that the liberty of the subjects is to be respected, less sacred than those which protect their lives? Will he whom sordid interest induces to violate the first, not only without scruple, but with alacrity, will *he* hesitate to infringe the law, when solicited by an interest more pressing, by a bribe more seductive? And what shall we think of the virtue which only withstands temptation till you reach its price? Suppose the chiefs should give way to it, are the subalterns endowed with the same fortitude? And in case they give way to it, do not *silence, mystery*, and the *Bastille*, assure them no less of impunity than success? All buy their places, as I have shewn above. Now can it reasonably be supposed, that men who are ready to purchase the right of disgracing themselves by that infamous service, because it is lucrative, will be capable of refusing with obstinacy the temptation of rendering it still more lucrative, by an engagement for which they may be handsomely rewarded?

I insist on this idea, because for length of time it cruelly engaged, or rather distracted me; because among the inumerable reasons, that point out the propriety of the abolition of the Bastille or at least of its regimen, this is the most striking; A Soyereign activated by the best intentions may be so far deceived, as to think prisons of state in general, and the arbitrary mandates by which they are peopled, inseparable accessories of Government; and necessary to maintain the tranquility of the Public, no less than to vindicate the just prerogatives of the Crown: but there is none who could be persuaded, that it is his duty to delegate to the most despicable of his satellites, a power over the life of all his subjects, without exception, which he would be ashamed to arrogate to himself; yet have we demonstrated that such are the consequences resulting from the regimen of the Bastille.

(7) Page 90. It is not indeed the clock alone that Mr. *Raymond Gualbert de Sartines* has so ingenuously constructed. The inscription informs us, that he also planned the building where that machine is placed; a building that comprehends the kitchen, the baths of the Governor, the kennel of the turn-keys, and the rest of the pack, which they call the *Etat-major*, except the Governor; whose dwelling, as I before observed is without, though his kitchen and his Lady's baths are within[3]: there are some particulars relating to these baths, not less curious than those concerning the clock.

Whether a Governor's wife bathes here or there appears to be a matter of perfect indifference; and so indeed it should be: but in the Bastille the most trifling circumstance has its consequences, and those consequences are ever afflicting. Her Ladyship's bathing-tub being situated in the interior part of the Bastille, in order to get to it, she must necessarily cross the court, the only place the prisoners are allowed to walk in. But her lackeys have to carry the water; they must pass in and out; and every time they pass, the prisoner, who is walking, gets an order to shut himself up in the closet.

Then arrive my Lady's maids: they must carry her Ladyship's linen, napkins, slippers, &c. The consequences would be dreadful, if a captive discovered the most minute of these *State-secrets*: each importation produces then another *closetting*.

---

[3] A new kitchen and baths were later built outside — in 1786? - the gate of the main castle, to one side of the path that faced the governor's house. (Bournon, 29, 31). See Appendix B.

At length Madam herself arrives: she is of no small weight: her gait is stately, and the place she has to pass through is of tolerable extent. The sentinel, in order to make his court, and to recommend himself for his alacrity, cries out, *To the Closet*. The moment he perceives her: the ambulating prisoner must fly, and remain in the closet till she has reached her bathing-place; and when she comes out again, her retreat is accompanied with the same formalities. The prisoner must in the same manner await in the closet the passage of the Mistress, the Chamber-maids and the Lackeys.

In my time a sentinel, on one of these occasions, having neglected to throw out the signal for flight, the modern *Diana*[48] was seen in her dishabille. I was the Acteon of the day: however, I underwent no metamorphosis; but the unlucky Soldier was imprisoned for eight days of which I could not be ignorant, having myself heard the order given for his confinement. In other places the baths confer either health or pleasure. A Governess of the Bastille is never seized with a fit of cleanliness, which does not cause in others several of vexation.

(8) *Page 95*. We have spoken in the text of the prisoner's *food*. As to the *clothing*, the Governor has often boasted to me of his liberality in this particular I do not think he ever honoured me with a visit, that he did not speak of *Breeches*, which he generously distributed to HIS PRISONERS; for in naming them he always used the possessive term. This is what I myself experienced.

I was taken into custody on the 27th of September on my way to dine in the country, and consequently had on the clothes one might be naturally expected to wear on such an expedition, in that season of the year. I could not possibly procure any fresh supply either of clothes or linen, till the conclusion of the November following. During that month, which in 1780 was extremely rigorous, I was reduced to the necessity of either condemning myself to close confinement in my cell, or of going naked, literally naked, to brave in my walk the violence of the cold; not-withstanding I had money, as I have already said, deposited in the hands of the officers;

and all I asked was liberty to *buy* the breeches which, I was informed, they *gave* to others.

But further: they sent me about the latter end of November, a winter collection from Mr. *Le Quesne's*. It consisted of stockings, which a child of fix years could scarcely have got on, with the rest of the habiliments in the same proportion. Doubtless they concluded I must have fallen away prodigiously. This may appear puerile to those who do not reflect upon circumstances: but here is another, that cannot appear so to anyone. I made grievous complaints at being derided in this manner; and begged the Governor would send back that child bedding, and supply me with something more suitable, or give me leave to purchase it. He answered me roundly, in presence of his Colleagues and a Turn-key, *that I might go to the .... that he did not care a .... about my breeches; that I should either have been aware of getting into the Bastille, or else I should learn to bear my sufferings when I was there*[*].

I confess, his comrades seemed to feel for him; and that eight days after, I got a morning-gown and a pair of breeches.

If these cruelties and insults, atrocious beyond conception, were not the consequence of Ministerial orders, I ought to publish them, in order that my successors may be exempted from them: if they were authorized, either by the rules of the prison or by the particular directions given for my treatment, it is still my duty to publish them, in order that the punctual Governor may not fail of meeting with the reward which he deserves for his diligence[BST].

---

[*] "Que je pouvois m'aller faire f..... qu'il se f.... bien de mes cullottes; . qu'il falloit ne pas se mettre dans le cas d'être a la Bastille, ou savoir souffrir quand on *y* etoit."

[BST] The 'reward' which De Launay ultimately got was to be massacred by the crowd that stormed the Bastille. One wonders if Linguet's words played any part, however distant, in the crowd's summary 'sentence'.

CONCLUSION.

I BEGIN to be tired of this gloomy subject, although it is yet far from being exhausted. I have here detailed only what has happened to myself, or what I might relate without hazarding the sources whence I derived my intelligence. What then would it be thought, if I revealed all that I learnt, either from the confidence or indiscretion of individuals, or from the sagacity with which the mind of a captive is inspired by the impossibility of amusing himself any other way than by endeavoring to penetrate the mysteries that surround him, which are so eagerly concealed from his inspection?

While these Memoirs were in the press, I received a book sent to me on the same subject, entitled, *Of Lettres-de-cachet, &c.* I am sorry it is anonymous, because that circumstance seems to derogate from its authenticity[1]. That book develops the mysteries of the Dungeon of *Vincennes*, as this does those of the *Bastille*. The reader may compare them: probably, in time, we may have separate histories of the several *Bastilles* which France contains, or rather which contain France in subjection.

All will justify the reflexion with which we began this melancholy narration; a reflexion that cannot too often be suggested to an equitable government, which is neither cruel through interest, nor through design. What is the object of that secrecy, that impenetrable reserve, that barbarity which characterize the prisons they pretend to call *Royal?* Every thing being done in the *King's name,* should it not the rather wear the appearance of clemency, or at least of justice? The rigours are not there subjected to any preliminary formality; the alleviations therefore should not be the more restrained.

But even if they contained in fact: none but real *State-criminals,* or men *really suspected* of having been concerned in practices against the State, yet even *they* should experience, till their conviction, the regard due to humanity. Let us not lose sight of that precious axiom in the Declaration of the 30th of

August 1780[2]; let us not forget the homage then paid by decency to truth. All punishments inflicted *in obscurity* are at least *useless.* Now, in the language of justice, what is an *useless punishment?* and what name is to be given to those useless punishments, when it is found that they fall on the innocent alone?

Once more, these *State-prisons,* these *State-tortures,* these *State-punishments,* are consigned to none less than to *Prisoners of State.* If the twenty or thirty jails, which in France bear that horrid name, if the showers of *Lettres-de-cachet* that fill them, served in reality only to repress faction, and to disconcert rebellion, the kingdom must necessarily be full of *Catilines*[3]. That country, where, of all in the universe, the yoke is born with the most patient docility, must then be a mere seminary for treason, and a very nest of conspirators: a supposition no less absurd than scandalous.

But if it is not the guilty who are heaped into *the Bastilles,* with what description of persons do they overflow? Whom does that dreadful apparatus threaten? For whom, then are reserved those dungeons, where silence is only interrupted by sighs, where terror watches to drive away all that might dissipate vexation? Alas! They are reserved for Fathers of families, and Citizens of irreproachable character; for Men of worth and probity, to whom Government perhaps owed gratitude and recompense.

Amongst a thousand generical examples perhaps a specific one may be required. Let us cite that of Mr. *De Bure*[BST], who has already had a place assigned him in the Annals[*BST2]. This man was a Bookseller of note: his family had carried on, for

---

[BST] Several De Bures appear as printers in Paris all through the eighteenth and into the nineteenth century. This was Guillaume De Bure, a highly respected bookseller. Increasing pressure was put on him to, effectively, become an informer – that is, to work with a police inspector to stamp works counterfeited by his colleagues. When he was finally put in the Bastille, his colleagues protested. When the Parlement of Paris threatened to call Lenoir (the Lieutenant of Police) before them to justify the imprisonment, he was released. Arnould, VI, 150.

[*] Vol. III, p. 239

[BST2] This item in the Annals resumes De Bure's story, essentially as told in the note above.

the space of a hundred years, from Father to Son, a business useful and deserving of encouragement, provided the professor be no less scrupulous than intelligent. He was at the head of the Society.

The Sovereign thinks proper to introduce a new police into that Corps. A law prescribes, that certain books shall be *stamped*, that is, have a mark impressed on them, to denote certain privileges allowed them. So far all went on well, particularly for those to whom this *stamping* would be highly profitable.

But a particular order enjoins Mr. *De Bure* himself to apply the stamp; to be the minister and manual executor of an operation, in which he foresees the infallible ruin of several families belonging to the company of which he is the head: he thinks that his conscience, no less than his honour, calls upon him to decline it: he offers his resignation, that an office repugnant to his disposition may pass into hands more tractable and docile.

His resignation is refused: they repeat a second, and a third time, STAMP! OR ELSE. . . . . He persists in his denial: they fulfill the alternative, and put him in the BASTILLE. Now that is what they call a STATE CRIMINAL.

THE END.

END NOTES

PART I

1 "It is my lot today, yours to-morrow" or, "Today me, tomorrow you".
2 Traditionally, the river of forgetfulness, though Greek sources had it variously as a being, a place or a plain, all with similar associations. *Oxford*, 322.
3 Dellon, a French doctor was arrested in Goa and held by the Inquisition there. He wrote a book about the experience despite the forced promise not to speak of the experience (see Bibliography).
4 Charles Gravier, count of Vergennes (1717-1787). Made foreign minister in 1774. A supporter of the American Revolution, he signed the alliance with Benjamin Franklin in February 6, 1778 and was the chief French representative at the peace negotiations at the end of the war. www.encyclopedia.com. A note in the *Biographie Universelle* praises him as a superior, if not a great, man of his time, wise, upright and hardworking, but also says "He hid his lack of sincerity under an air of candor and simplicity." *Biographie universelle*, XLIII, 153n. His responses to Linguet might be viewed as cases in point.
5 Jean-Frédéric Phelippeaux, Count of Maurepas (1701- 1781), from old nobility, was Secretary of State at twenty-four. Marmontel called him "the most seductive of ministers". A charming and witty, if mediocre, man, he served as Secretary of State under Louis XV before being disgraced for a four-line satire on Madame Pompadour. Louis XVI brought him back in 1774 until his death in 1781. *Biographie universelle*, XXVII, 335-339.
6 An exempt here was a kind of policeman, often sent to execute an arrest or other order.
7 Linguet claimed to have invented a telegraph, and is sometimes listed as one of several early originators of that device. He gave no details though the reference here to light suggests that would have been the signaling medium.
8 A town between Rheims and Paris in the Champagne region. Cardinal Mazarin bought the duchy of Rethel and his title was confirmed in 1663, which is why Linguet later refers to it as "Rethel Mazarine". Despite Linguet's dismissal, the Encyclopedia says it was one of the finest duchies in the kingdom. *Encyclopédie*, Tome 14, 203.
9 The Holy Roman Empire.
10 Rumor at least supports this. When the Academy tried to have the *Annales* banned in 1778, Amelot was said to have answered, "I am sorry, Messieurs, I cannot agree to your demand. The King, the Queen and the whole royal family read only Linguet's paper, and read it with indescribable pleasure." Apparently he only gave up this pleasure with regret: "October 14, 1780. – The King has just twice sacrificed almost at the same time both his tastes and his personal affections to the desires of his counsel, and apparently for the good of the state. It is well-known that Linguet's Annals was the only paper he read. He read it with pleasure and supported this writer at a time when a truly reprehensible license removed all limits to his satirical touches, whose glow reflected even on Royalty itself. Now here he is locked up." *Correspondance Secrète*, I, 133, 320.
11 The passage from the *Annales* Linguet cites in his note explains why, despite the generous reception he had found in England, he felt it necessary to leave as war approached.

SECTION II
12 Presumably Marie-Antoinette, wife of Louis XVI and sister of Joseph II.
13 Emmanuel Felicité de Durfort, Duc de Duras (1715-1789) - Marshal of France, 1775 (one of 20 named by Louis XIV), member of the French Academy, 1775, Secretary of State, 1767. A literate and apparently modern man whom one peddler of forbidden books named as a customer. *Mémoires de Linguet*, 212. Bachaumont. "He said he had been the partisan, the admirer, the defender of the journalist; to the point that he made himself the peddler of Linguet's pages; but... if he had him in hand he would kill him." Bachaumont also preserves the beginning of the letter in question: "There is a lot of talk about a handwritten letter to the Marshal the Duke of Duras which begins: 'Who are you, to have the right to question me,' etc.? But since nobody claims to have read it, and it hasn't been made public, one can always doubt the fact." Linguet's papers were dispersed or destroyed after his arrest under the Terror, and this letter with them. Bachaumont, XVI, 16-17; XX, 260.
14 The Count Desgrée du Lou was a Breton count who had been, several times, president of the Breton Nobility during a period when it was defying royal authority. Having learned that Duras claimed he'd taken a bribe to betray his group's interests, he responded with an indignant letter. Proofs and counter-proofs, memoirs and counter-memoirs followed. Linguet, having first told this story in the *Annales*, later expressed surprise that the conflict continued and wrote an update which in effect said that, the amount being minimal (1500 pounds), the whole exchange was beneath the dignity of both parties. *Annales* – (1777) 1779, 57-64, 189-194.
15 Jean-Jacques Du Val d'Eprémesnil (1746-1794). His uncle, Georges du Val de Leyrit (1715-1764), was the French governor in India when General Lally (see note on page 5151) surrendered Pondicherry. In defending him, Lally's son inevitably attacked Leyrit, whom d'Eprémesnil in turn defended, often thwarting Lally-Tollendal's efforts. *Biographie Universelle*, XII, 524-529; XXIV, 428-433.
16 Presumably a work by Duras. Linguet's manner of referring to it and the fact that it is not readily identifiable suggest that it was less than memorable.
17 The Secretaries Linguet refers to were very much like law clerks. The article in question ("Difficulties arising in the French Parliament", 222) attacks various aspects of the French Parliament – unthinkable if Linguet had been in France at the time -, including the fact that the Secretaries were paid by the public, rather than the government, leading to abuses. *Annales*, Tome 8 (1780), 234-238. (The numbering Linguet refers to is not at all clear in the originals – in this case, the article appears in N° 60, which appears *after* 61.)
18 A Marshal of France (there were several) was one of the Great Officers of the Crown of France and took precedence over the Constable of France.
19 See note 18 to Section III for more about this idea.
20 Frederick the Great.
21 This 'Epistle to M. Alembert' appears in the *Annales* as a poem that goes on for several sarcasm-filled pages. *Annales*, Tome 9 (1778), 79-86.
22 Briefly, a miller in Prussia complained that the water upstream from his mill had been diverted. Though this seems not to have been the case, the issue escalated all the way up to Frederick, who accused his subordinates of covering

for each other and ended up removing a minister who was not even involved. *Annales*, Tome 9 (1778), 4-16.

23 That is, the so-called Philosophers, who didn't care for Linguet any more than he cared for them.

24 This passage in the *Annales* quotes a statement by Frederick following the affair of the Miller (see note above) in which he says that "a tribunal that commits injustices is more dangerous than a band of thieves" since at least one can defend oneself against thieves. This language closely resembles Linguet himself had used, and quotes. *Annales*, Tome 7 (1779), 434.

25 Callisthenes (c.370-327 BC) was an historian who (extravagantly) praised Alexander the Great, but later quarrelled with him and was put to death.

26 "Arise and Walk". In Matthew 9:5, Jesus says this to a man sick of the palsy: "For whether it is easier, to say, Thy sins be forgiven thee; or to say, Arise, and walk?"

NOTES

1 Jacques Necker (1732-1804), a Swiss-born banker who became France's minister of finance three times (1776-1781, 1788-89 and 1789-90). His attempts at reform twice led to his dismissal; he resigned the third time. *Benet's*, 722. "His dismissal contributed to the public mind which culminated in the storming of the Bastille". *Chambers*, 1353.

2 Berville and Barrière point out that Linguet's version is correct, except on two essential points – Sully never spoke of the Bastille (he basically told the king, "If you'd only listened to me") and in fact he was deeply pained by Henri's passion for the Prince's wife. *Mémoires de Linguet*, 228.

3 When people had descended into this cave to consult an oracle, it was said that they were so awe-struck they never smiled again.

4 The Robe and the Sword; that is, men of law and men of the military.

5 The Master of Requests was originally responsible for managing pleas to the king (who had once accepted them directly), but the office became a complex mix, described by Cotgrave (in 1611) as follows: "They be Conseillers of the bodie of Parlement, and of the great Counsell, over which in the absence of the Judges, they preside, as they do also at the Seates of all Parlementall Chaunceries, where they hear the reports of the Referenderies: they also take notice of the falsification of Chauncerie Seales; and judge... all controversies arising about the Titles of all royal Offices." For a longer account of this office and its evolution, see Chéruel, II, 717-718.

6 The tax "farm" referred to a system by which individuals collected taxes for the king – not incidentally keeping some for themselves. The Revolution ended this system. Chéruel, I, 415.

7 The Chancellor's office went back to Roman times and was revived after the Revolution until 1848. The Chancellor was chief among the Great Officers of the Crown and presided at councils and in Parlement. He fixed the royal seal to all letters and other documents from the king, but could refuse when he found them contrary to the kingdom's laws. Chéruel, I, 129.

8 See note on page 51.

9 The chief tribunal of Paris. Cheruel, I, 140.

10 That is, a King's Commissioner; a very general term for anyone executing a wide range of political, legal or other commissions for the king. Cheruel, I, 187.

11 See the discussion in the introduction ("About Linguet") of how Linguet angered Vergennes and others. The letter itself became a clandestine best seller for a number of booksellers. Darnton, 48, 64.
12 Pierre Le Quesne, a merchant of silk cloth (on the Rue Bourdonnois in Paris) who represented the *Annales* in France. *Annales*, Tome IX, January 1783, 449-472.
13 The Adhémar de Panat family still exists today. Several members played a part in French history around this time. The reference might be to François-Louis Adhémar, Count of Panat (?-1792), who was later a deputy from the nobility of Rouergue to the Estates General in 1789 and signed a protest against revolutionary innovations. *Biographie universelle* I, 178.
14 This is in Tome IX, January 1783, 449-472. It anticipates the current work in a number of ways, but also formally declares that Du Quesne no longer represents the journal and says frankly that this silk merchant was a police spy (which Linguet deduces from the fact that, having invited him to dinner, Du Quesne literally delivered him to the Bastille.)
15 "Thus do they live there".
16 These are some of the pleasures of Paris of the time, including the Champs-Elysées and the *Mercure Galant*, a well-known newspaper.

SECTION III
1 The Ephori were five magistrates in Sparta who had power over even its King.
2 *Robinson Crusoe* (1719) and *Gulliver's Travels* (1726) are the two most famous examples.
3 James Cook's voyages of exploration (1768-1771, 1772-1775 and 1776-1780) are well-known. George Anson's six ships attacked Spanish settlements from 1740-1744, bringing back 400,000 pounds in Spanish booty, but losing over one thousand sailors to scurvy, prompting the search for a cure.
4 See note on page 39.
5 The standard criminal procedure in old regime France was anything but open. Jousse, in his guide to French law of the time, has several pages on the secrecy of procedure. Jousse, Partie III, Livre III, Titre II, p. 145-148. Even when every French institution was being reexamined as the Revolution got underway, at least one writer defended this secrecy, in part because it kept people from influencing witnesses' statements, but also because it kept people from sparing the accused out of pity for his or her family (who would share in any disgrace). Mézard, 22-23.
6 Or his 'accomplice' (*compère*), says the *Biographie Universelle*. Louis Tristan (14th c., dates unknown) was Louis XI's Grand Provost – something more than a mere executioner – and did his dirty work. Some say he had over 4000 people thrown into rivers sewn in sacks. *Biographie universelle* XVII, 173.
7 Louis Phelippeaux, count de Florentin, later duke de la Vrillière (1705-1777). Louis XV valued his services and he was popular for a time with the public. *Biographie Universelle,* XXXVII, 313. Dumouriez calls him "the most base and the most permanent of Louis XV's ministers". II, 285.

8 Louis XVI's brothers: Monsieur was the Count of Provence (1733-1824), later Louis XVIII (1794-1824) and the Count of Artois (1757-1836) was later Charles X (1824-1830). *Biographie universelle* XXV, 239-260; VII 543-559.

9 Caligula "generally prolonged the sufferings of his victims by causing them to be inflicted by slight and frequently repeated strokes; this being his well-known and constant order: "Strike so that he may feel himself die." C. Suetonius, 272-273, XXX.

10 Figures from Greek mythology punished in memorable ways: Tantalus was condemned to have wonderful fruits and other delights all around him that withdrew when he reached for them; Ixion was bound to a burning wheel that spun in space; Sisyphus was made to roll a rock uphill that kept coming back down as he reached the top.

11 Diderot's *Encyclopédie* says juniper was burned to purify the air. VII, 581.

12 Phalaris was a Sicilian tyrant (570-554 BC) known for putting people in a brass bull and heating it so that their cries became the bull's 'bellows'.

13 "Cell of prison where the prisoner pays his own comforts." *Le Grand Dictionnaire Terminologique*. It was also a common French and Spanish coin.

14 Antoine-Jean Amelot de Chaillou (1732-1795), Secretary of State 1776-1783.

15 The grove, first a gymnasium, where Arisotle taught. *Oxford,* 334.

16 Linguet had been a lawyer and so in theory speaks here with some authority. But the secrecy of Old Regime procedure was a given. Max Gallo: "Keeping the accusation secret is the key to this procedure. The ignorance in which the accused is kept gives the judge a free hand and disorients the accused." Gallo, 143. Linguet himself had criticized it, just years before: "...justice, by the voluntary obscurity in which it wraps itself...[removes] all means of being illuminated. How is it that this odious mystery, of which everybody feels the abuse and the danger, of which magistrates themselves wish and request the reform, is still upheld? Each detests it: each feels, in detail, its inconveniences; everywhere its absurdity is deplored; and nonetheless it continues to make victims every year!" *Annales*, Tome 3, 1777, 321.

17 Referring to Sartine, and suggesting that his experience as head of the secret police colored his approach to running the Navy.

18 Linguet was not alone in believing this. Boissy d'Anglas said the Duke de la Vrillière (originally the Count de Saint-Florentin) "was responsible for the distribution of *lettres-de-cachet*: and the imagination recoils at the immense number he signed: he distributed them by the thousands... it is said that he gave out more than fifty thousand during his ministry: this number seems exaggerated at first, but in reflecting on the ease with which they were given, and even the shameful commerce which people did not blush to make of them, one can believe that it is not". Count Boissy-d'Anglas, *Essai,* cited in *Mémoires de Linguet,* 184. Funck-Brentano, having read through the Bastille's archives and a number of later studies of lettres-de-cachet, concluded that it was, for the most part, a myth. By his account, blank letters did exist, but were only issued in very limited numbers to Intendants and other highly placed officials and then mainly because they were too far from Paris to allow nominal letters to be issued in crisis situations. In general, too, letters were not given out to family members. Funck-Brentano, 35-40. Chassaigne largely confirms this in an article exploring the use of letters-de-cachet as an extension of traditional paternal authority. Chassaigne, 562-576, continued in 1905 issue, 60-73.

19 The end of judicial torture in France was declared on August 24, 1780 - up to a point: "In the French sources ordinary judicial torture is known as *torture préparatoire*, as opposed to this torture of a convict, so-called *torture préalable*, literally "preliminary torture" in the sense of being preliminary to the execution of the capital sentence. The safeguards of the ordinary law of torture, such as the requirement of probable cause, did not exist. Torture préalable was regarded as much less objectionable than ordinary judicial torture. Even Voltaire defended it. When Louis XVI abolished 'ordinary' judicial torture in 1780, he excepted torture préalable until 1788." Langbein, 17.

LINGUET'S NOTES
20 Presumably refers to the admired Roman emperor Titus Flavius Vespasianus, who ruled 79-81.
21 Dionysius I (?-367 BC) was sole ruler of Syracuse from 405-367, and was considered effective, but oppressive. *Oxford*, 546.
22 Linguet uses the term 'lettre-de-cachet' loosely here to refer to various acts of royal authority. Ironically, in doing so, he echoes the author of a pamphlet contesting the current work, which said, in effect, that though other countries did not have usually have letters-de-cachet per se, they had – with the exception of England - the equivalent, often in no more than a word from the ruler. Even the Pope could send someone to the galleys with documents carrying the phrase "Such is our pleasure". *Observations sur l'Histoire de la Bastille publiée par Linguet*, 83, cited in *Mémoires de Linguet*, 187-189.
23 All three assisted emperors, with varying degrees of violence. Lucius Aelius Sejanus (?-AD 29?), chief of the prætorian guard under Tiberius (14-29), gathered increasing personal power, but was executed in 29. Narcissus (?-AD 54), a freedman, prospered as the emperor Claudius' private secretary, but was forced to commit suicide by Nero. Tigellinus (?-AD 69) was most known for his part in Nero's executions, as head of the prætorian guard (62-8). *Oxford*, 571.
24 Seneca (4 BC-AD 65) was a Roman Stoic philosopher who became Nero's tutor and advisor, but ultimately plotted to assassinate him and was commanded to kill himself, which he did, by opening his veins. *Benet's*, 929. Publius Clodius Thrasea Paetus (?-AD 66) was a Stoic senator who was forced to commit suicide during Nero's reign. *Oxford*, 569.
25 Cornelius Tacitus (AD 55?-117), the great Roman historian, whose works include *Historiae*, the *Annales* and *Germania*. *Benet's*, 1002.
26 "Eorum qui de se statuebant humabantur corpora, manebant testamenta, pretium festinandi (Those who passed sentence on themselves were rewarded for their dispatch by being allowed burial and having their wills respected). Tacitus, *Annals*, VI (29)" Cited in Montesquieu, p. 118.
27 Seajanus' body was, it is said, torn to pieces after his execution and thrown in the Tiber. *Oxford*, 514.
28 These were some of the most benevolent Roman emperors. Trajan (Marius Uplius Traiainus) (53?-117) was emperor from 98 to 117 and the Antonines – Antoninus Pius (86-161, ruled 138-161), Marcus Aurelius (121-180, ruled 161-180) and Commodus (161-192, ruled 180-192) – ruled during the long period of prosperity called the Age of the Antonines (138-192). *Oxford*, 41, 578.

29 It is not clear what Linguet means here, since the elder Agrippa (Marcus Vipsanius Agrippa, 64-12 BC), Augustus's right-hand man) died before Tiberius' reign and the younger (Marcus Vipsanius Agrippa Postumus (12 BC-AD14) was murdered as soon as Tiberius took power. *Oxford*, 19.

30 Roman law included several degrees of exile, the most severe being *deportatio*, transportation (generally to an island), which included loss of civil rights, and usually of property. *Oxford*, 229; Seyffert,182-183.

31 Constantine I, the Great (Flavius Valerius Constantinus Augustus) (c. 285-337). Though he did have these people killed, his use of baths as a weapon has been called into doubt. *Oxford*, 154; Smith, 835.

32 Constantius II (317-361, sole emperor 353-361). Smith, 831. The letter writer was probably Luciferus I of Cagliari (in Sardinia), a combative bishop whose willingness to abrasively confront authority recalls Linguet himself. "[In his books and pamphlets] Lucifer addresses Constantius... with a remarkable vigour of denunciation. He evidently courted persecution, and even martyrdom." Rev. J. Ll. Davies, D. Litt, "Luciferus I., bishop of Calaris" in *A Dictionary of Christian Biography and Literature to the End of the Sixth Century* (web version).

33 St. John Chrysostom (344?-407). Called 'Chrysostom' (golden-mouthed) for his eloquence. He died while en route to Pythius, where he had been exiled.

34 The Prison of the Seven Towers, or Yedikule, is still a tourist attraction today. "Istanbul – Off the Beaten Track", *Lonely Planet*, web site.

35 Many Christians captured as slaves were ransomed. In one example among many, Bachaumont describes, on October 24, 1785, a procession of "three hundred thirteen French slaves, redeemed in Alger in 1785, by the two orders of the Redemption...The custom is to promenade and to show these slaves to excite first the curiosity and then the charity of the public." Tome 30, 24.

36 Selictar-Aga, a high official in the Ottoman empire whose ceremonial role was to carry the sultan's sword. Rycaut, 54.

37 The Ottoman empire.

38 A civil war had just begun in Persia with the death of Karim Khan Zand and would last until 1794.

39 Though translated here, the French word – *cangue* – is more widely used. An image of an Uzbek prisoner from the Album of the Amir of Bukhara shows a forked stick wedged against the man's neck, with a strap holding his left wrist. Grube, 92, plate 71. Richard Burton describes the cangue's Chinese origin: "Arab. "Al-bayt" = the house. The Arabs had probably learned this pleasant mode of confinement from the Chinese whose Kea or Cangue is well known. The Arabian form of it is "Ghull," or portable pillory, which reprobates will wear on Judgment Day." *The Book Of The Thousand Nights And A Night*, Volume 5 , fn #481. Numerous images of the Chinese version show it as a platform locked around the neck (sometimes of several people at once). - Ghengis Khan was even subject to "the indignity of the cangue." "CHAPTER V - THE MONGOL CONQUEST OF CHINA" web site. Examples have also been found in ancient Greece. "Prisonnier /Des prisonniers torturés ou executes", *Electre* web site.

40 Though Christians and finally all foreigners except the Dutch were banned from Japan through the early seventeenth century, interest in the West was in fact reawakening in the eighteenth century.

41 Yong Zheng, reign 1722-1736 AD, was the third Emperor of the Qing Dynasty, who banned Christianity early in his reign.
42 Ouida, a coastal town in Benin most known for its role in the slave trade.
43 An alternate version of 'Christian'; in this case, Christian II, King of Denmark and Norway 1513-23 and Sweden 1520-23. "As he himself said, the toughest medicine best cures the illness". Responsible for the Stockholm Massacre in 1520, in which a number of Swedish nobles and bishops were executed despite the king's having promised them all amnesty. www.danskekonger.dk/eng/biografi/ChrII.html.
44 Once the Roman emperor Hadrian's tomb, it was already known in Linguet's time as the Castel Sant'Angelo. Still a popular tourist attraction. A tourist guide said in 1778: "It is in this castle that are prisoners of state." Magnan, 55.
45 Louis François I de Bourbon (1717-1776), Prince of Conti 1727-1776.
46 Marie-Marguerite Marquise de Brinvilliers (?-1676) was one of the great criminals of Louis XIV's reign. A beautiful petite aristocrat, she poisoned a number of people, some apparently for practice or by a misplaced benevolence. (One young woman was spared a life in a convent when her parents mysteriously died.) The resulting scandal was known as "The Affair of the Poisons". *Biographie Universelle*, Tome V, 546-549.
47 The Statute of 1670 (*Ordonnance de 1670*), which was the basis for most French criminal laws through the 18th century, says: "The accused people who have been arrested will be immediately taken to prison, without being detained in private houses." Title 13, article 38.
48 When the hunter Acteon accidentally saw the goddess Diana naked, she changed him into a hart and his own hounds killed him.

CONCLUSION
1 Its author today is far better known than Linguet. This is Mirabeau's *Des lettres de cachet et des prisons d'état*, which was as successful at the time as Linguet's work.
2 The English edition used here does not include this statement, which is quoted at the start of the French edition: "These unknown sufferings and these obscure punishments, from the moment they do not contribute to maintaining order by publicity and by example, become useless to our justice."
3 Lucius Sergius Catalina (?-62 BC) was a Roman patrician who led a famous conspiracy which was uncovered by Cicero and defeated. *Oxford*, 119.

APPENDICES

APPENDIX A. INTAKE AND EXIT FORMS

Bureaucracy has a long history in France. Even the Bastille, extra-legal as it may seem to us today, had its standard procedures and forms, including these two for a prisoner's arrival and (less certain) departure.

Standard Entry Form

This day the (day, month, year), Sir _____ has entered the Bastille by order of the king, brought by Sir _____. Sir _____ had on him, in gold as well as silver, jewels, etc. _____ and concerning any papers, we have put them in an envelope, sealed with the castle's seal, or his own (if he has one) : (he may keep his seal) which package he has labeled around his seal and signed with his hand. In regards to his sword, its appearance is described. Sir _____ having no other effects on him, has signed the said entry, day, month and year as above.—If the officer has affixed a seal, or several, this is indicated at the bottom of the said entry.

Standard Exit (or Liberty) Form
Order counter-signed by _____ on the date of _____

The _____ being freed, I promise, in accordance with the king's orders, to not speak to anyone at all, in any manner whatsoever, of the prisoners, nor anything else concerning the castle of the Bastille, of which I might have knowledge. Further, I acknowledge that all gold, silver, paper, effects and jewels which I brought with me or have had brought to the said castle during the time of my detention have been returned to me: in witness of which I have signed the present document.

At the castle of the Bastille (day, month, year) at _____ o'clock.

(*Bastille devoilée*, I, cited in *Mémoires de Linguet*, 184)

APPENDIX B. THE LAYOUT OF THE BASTILLE

For a modern reader to visualize the Bastille as it appeared to most Parisians, it is probably simplest to realize that if you had looked up the Rue St. Antoine (still a major thoroughfare) towards where the Place de la Bastille is today, you would have seen two massive towers, joined by thick walls, dominating the view, with a space at left. (At the time, the Rue St. Antoine veered left along the castle's outer walls, then continued straight on to the Porte St. Antoine.) These were joined to two others, visible at right, above various roofs and steeples. Otherwise, for a more detailed sense of the physical Bastille, Berville and Barrière provide a long history and description from the *Bastille devoilée* which includes this overview of the castle's layout:

> The entry of the Bastille...[was] at right of the far end of the Rue St. Antoine; above the first gate was a considerable storeroom of weapons of different sorts, and of old armor; next to this gate was a guard house where two sentries were placed each night, to respond and open to people who appeared. This gate led to a first exterior courtyard in which were the barracks for invalid soldiers, stables and storerooms for the governor. One could equally access this courtyard from the arsenal. It was separated from a second courtyard by a gate next to which was another guard house, by a ditch and a drawbridge. The governor's townhouse was in this second courtyard, at right. Facing this townhouse was an avenue fifteen *toises* [*about ninety feet*] long, whose right side was bordered by a building serving as a kitchen; in this same structure was a bathroom, built in recent years for the use of the governor's wife. All this was on a ... bridge which crossed the main ditch and on which a drawbridge was lowered beyond which was another guardhouse. This led to the large interior courtyard. To access this,... it was still necessary to go through a strong set of bars, which served as an entrenchment to the sentry, who was under orders not to let any of the prisoners approach it within three feet. This large courtyard was two hundred feet long by seventy-two wide; it was bordered by the towers called *de la Liberté*,

de la Bertaudière, de la Bazinière, de la Comté, du Trésor, de la Chapelle and the solid walls which joined these six towers.... This courtyard ended in a modern building, which an inscription in letters of gold, on black marble placed above the door, proclaimed to have been built in 1761, under the reign of Louis XV, and under the ministry of M. Phelippeaux de Saint-Florentin, minister of Paris, by M. de Sartine, then lieutenant of police, for the lodging of staff officers. It had been built on a very different model from the rest, and had more the air of a rich individual's house that that of a supplement to horrible prisons. The lower part of this building was occupied by the council chamber, by toilets, kitchens, a laundry, etc., which had exits on the rear courtyard, and by the lodgings of subaltern officers and turn-keys. At right, on the second floor, above the council chamber, was the apartment of the king's lieutenant; on the third, that of the major; on the fourth, that of the surgeon. The rest of these three upper floors were occupied by a certain number of rooms destined for very distinguished prisoners, et to sick people who required care... In times of crowding, all the rooms in this house, the antechambers, the chambers, even the cabinets of the staff officers were filled with prisoners. The second courtyard was bordered by this same modern-style building, [and] by the towers called *du Puits* and *du Coin* and the corresponding walls. Between the two towers... were rooms occupied by the kitchen help, and some prisons used only in case of need. This courtyard was the lower court of the castle; it was used in former times for the kitchen trash, and poultry were raised there.

(from *La Bastille devoilée*, 2nd delivery, cited in *Mémoires de Linguet*, 239-243)

Coeuret gives some additional notes: The 'distinguished prisoners' put in the modern building often had been sent there by their families. The same building held a library. Archives were kept on piles along the wall between the *Bartaudière* and the *Bazinière*. The 'Closet' (*Cabinet*) mentioned by Linguet was a low, dark room at right, between the *Trésor* and the *Chapelle*. The detritus in the Courtyard of the *Puits* made it a source of infection. (Coueret, 46-53).

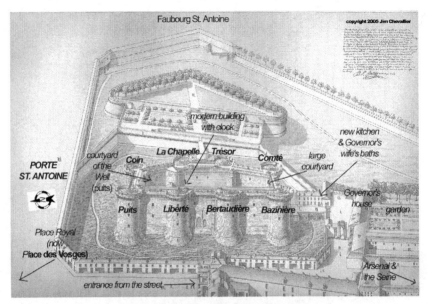

View of the Bastille from the west

Views of the Bastille showing the towers and their names, directions to some landmarks and other significant details. The original 19th century images show the castle in 1789 (above) with the new kitchen and baths (built in 1786) and in 1650 (below) without them.

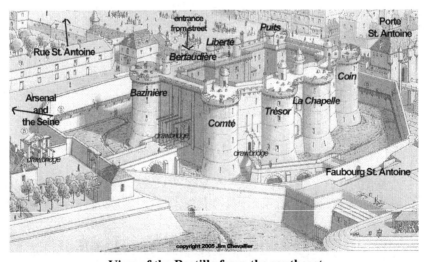

View of the Bastille from the southeast

All of the towers' names but one can be simply explained:

- The *Tour du Coin* ("Tower of the Corner") was near the corner of the Rue St. Antoine. Linguet was in N° 2 of this tower.
- The *Tour de la Chapelle* ("Tower of the Chapel") once held the old chapel, later replaced by one on the opposite side (between the Liberty and *Bertaudière* towers, where, Linguet complains, it was crowned with a pigeon-house).
- The *Tour du Trésor* ("Tower of the Treasury") may have been where gold and silver had been stored when, in the past, Henri IV had money put in the Bastille for safekeeping. Pellissery was in N° 2 of this tower.
- The name of the *Tour du Comté* ("Tower of the County") has not been explained.
- The *Tour de la Bazinière* was probably named for M. de la Bazinière, held there in 1663. The Man in the (so-called) Iron Mask spent a few hours here when he arrived.
- The *Tour de la Bertaudière* was named for a mason, Bertaud, who fell from it while it was being build. This is where the Man in the Iron Mask spent his five years (1698-1703) in the Bastille.
- The *Tour de la Liberté* ("Tower of Freedom")'s grimly ironic name prompted this comment from Dumouriez "...by a refinement of barbary, this name was given to a tower of the Bastille." (II, 259). It was in fact the Parisian populace who named it, in one of the first popular assaults (there were several) on the Bastille, in 1380, when they cried out "Freedom! Freedom!" ("*Liberté, Liberté!*"). It also held the torture room for the Bastille, the subject of much rumor outside, but never mentioned by the memoirists I have consulted. (Torture was long

considered a normal tool of justice, not only in France but elsewhere.)
- The *Tour du Puits* ("Tower of the Well") was near the large well used by the kitchen.

(Coeuret, 46-48; *Mémoires de Linguet*, 241-243; Bournon, 294-295)

Appendix C. Food In the Bastille

One of the more common – and surprising – comments in memoirs of the Bastille is on the excellence of the meals. Even Linguet begrudgingly says, "There are tables less lacking; I confess it; mine was among them." General Dumouriez puts it succinctly: "One was very well fed at the Bastille, there were always five dishes for dinner, three for supper, without the dessert; which served all together, looked magnificent." (II, 289-290). The abbé Morellet describes more modest, but satisfying meals: "Each day I got a bottle of decent wine, an excellent one-pound loaf of bread; for dinner, a soup, some beef, an entrée and a dessert; in the evening, some roast and a salad." (I, 97). Marmontel gives a longer and somewhat more comic account:

> Two hours later, the locks of the two doors which locked me in wake me with their noise from a deep sleep, and two jailors, carrying a dinner which I think mine, and serve it in silence. One sets before the fire three small plates covered with dishes of common earthenware; the other unfolds, on the one table of two that is vacant, coarse but white linen. I see him put on this table a clean enough setting, spoon and fork of tin, a good household bread, a bottle of wine. Their service done, the jailors leave…
>
> Then Bury [*his servant*].. serves me soup: it was a Friday. This soup, for a fast day, was a purée of white broad beans, made with the freshest butter, and a dish of these same beans was the first Bury served me. I found all this very good. The dish of cod which he brought me for the second serving was even better, the little accent of garlic seasoned it with a delicacy of taste and odor which would have flattered the taste of the most gourmet Gascon; the wine wasn't excellent, but good enough; no dessert; one had to go without something. Besides, I found that one dined very well in the Bastille.
>
> As I rose from the table, and Bury prepared to sit down (because there was still enough for his dinner in what

remained), here came my two jailors with new dishes in hand. At the sight of this setting with good linen, on handsome earthenware, spoon and fork of silver, we realized our mistake, but we showed no sign of it, and once our jailors....were gone, Bury said: "Monsieur, you just ate my dinner; you won't mind if in my turn I eat yours." "Fair enough," I said and the walls of my room were, I think, astonished to hear laughter.

This dinner was of flesh: here are the details: an excellent soup, a succulent slice of beef, a boiled leg of capon, dripping with fat and falling off the bone; a small plate of fried artichokes in a marinade, one of spinach, a very nice *cresonne* pear, fresh grapes, a bottle of old Burgundy wine, and the best Moka coffee: this was Bury's dinner, except for the fruit and coffee which he gladly left for me.

...You have just seen how I was normally fed at the Bastille. (II, 133-135)

These last three prisoners, it should be said, were all among the best-treated. Several accounts give a less appetizing idea of the more normal fare:

a pound of bread and a bottle of bad wine a day; for dinner (at eleven o'clock in the morning), broth and two meat dishes; for supper (six o'clock in the evening), a slice of roast, some stew, and some salad, but all disgusting. Fast-day meals with rancid butter or sickening oil. - The diet of bread and water was only applied to common criminals."
(*la Bastille devoilée*, cited in Coeuret, 20)

Bread and water in fact seems to have been a punishment diet, used only in the dungeons.

De Junca, an official around the start of the century, said that one of his duties was to "watch the food one gives to prisoners, which is often bad, with bad wine and dirty linen." (Bournon, 269).

A prisoner who was being intentionally mistreated might get even worse. A man who was not only a Protestant (itself viewed as a stain) but had been accused of treason arrived in one of Renneville's cells in a terrible state and told him he'd only gotten "a little soup of boiled water and about two ounces of meat worse than what they give soldiers… and there are prisoners treated worse than me." (Savine, 87). (The phrase 'worse than what they give soldiers' occurs elsewhere, and gives some idea of how badly off the latter were.)

The bread and bottle of wine mentioned above, by the way, would have been offered as breakfast, as it was even for more favored prisoners from the seventeenth century (La Porte, 351) all the way to the later eighteenth century (Dumouriez, 259). It was served, as Linguet says, at seven. In the rest of France, this had been the standard breakfast at the start of the century but had already been largely replaced by coffee at this point. Though the Bastille administration may not have made the change because of the dangers associated with hot liquids, the prisoners were after all served soup and Marmontel mentions, above, getting coffee with another meal. The more likely cause was simply bureaucratic inertia.

A rare example of someone who went through various levels of treatment at the castle was Renneville, who frequently describes his own meals and those of others, starting right after his arrival:

> My dinner… consisted of a soup of green peas, garnished with lettuce, well simmered and appetizing, with a quarter of a fowl on it. In one dish, there was a succulent slice of beef with juice and a crown of parsley, and in another a quarter of *godiveau* [*a kind of minced meat pie*], well garnished with veal sweetmeats, cock's crests, asparagus, mushrooms, truffles, etc. and in another a sheeps' tongue in stew, all very well prepared and for dessert a biscuit and two Reinette apples…. My supper… consisted of a nice piece of roast veal with its juices, with two other dishes; in one of which was half a chicken and in the other a stew of *béatiles* [*that is, cock's crests, veal sweetbreads, paté garnish*]. With all this came a salad of hearts of lettuce, very well seasoned and, for desert, a dish of strawberries in wine and sugar. …

From May 16th until July 31, I was always treated in the same manner, but always with changes. That is, if today, I had a quarter of fowl in my soup, tomorrow it was a veal shank or a thick slice of mutton, always, some pastry, with little patés or a quarter *godiveau* In the evening... one day it was lamb or mutton with squab, another it was veal and half a chicken or a quarter of a capon and always a different stew with a salad and a dessert, all nicely served and very good. Every morning they brought me, for the day, a one-pound loaf of bread, cooked the day before, the finest in Paris, and a bottle of wine of about three half-*sétiers* for my dinner and the afternoon another for my supper. On fast days, I was even better treated then on meat days. For dinner, I had a good soup, sometimes of shrimp, of oysters, of mussels with a plate of very good fish, boiled, one roasted or fried and a dish of vegetables, such as asparagus, artichokes, peas, cauliflower if in season, as well as dessert. For the fish, either fresh or salt-water, I can say that it was the best of the fish market, often fresh salmon, weever, sole, perch, pike, trout, etc. In the best inns of Paris I could not have eaten better for a crown per meal. [But later.. they] gave me beef worse than what they give soldiers and awful vegetables, such as peas, broad beans, string bean, lentils and cooked in salt and water and yet the king paid the same price, a *pistole* a day, for my food....

The next day, Ru brought me my bread and wine as usual.... [For dinner] they'd cut back a good deal on my usual fare. I had, nonetheless, a good soup with croutons, a decent piece of beef, a mutton tongue in stew, and two *échaudés* for my dessert. I was served pretty much the same way the whole time I stayed in that miserable place. Sometimes they added a wing or a leg of fowl; sometimes two small pates, but often, I noticed that Ru had nibbled them, by the bits left on the edge of the plate. In the evening, I had roast veal or mutton with a little stew, sometimes a squab, and more sometimes more rarely, half a chicken and from time to time a salad....

[*After his cellmate gave a valuable ring to one of the jailors*] we ate very well. Pigeons, capons, game, sweets, pastry, dessert, Champagne and Burgundy wine, we lacked nothing. [*But once the man's rich father guaranteed payment, another jailer]* plucked the poor pigeon exorbitantly. He tried to pass off wine that had cost at most 6 sols a bottle for Champagne at 20 sols, nasty apples which would have revolted pigs for Reinette apples, small rotten chestnuts for those of Mans: tough old chicken for the wild chickens of Cottentin. [*Finally the cellmate said*]… that he allowed him to count double the price of things so long as he chose the best.

(Savine, 39, 43-44, 63, 83, 130)

When Renneville was in the dungeon for twenty–two days, the kindly Ru was horrified to find him there and soon after sent him: "a roast weever, a fried sole, a dish of asparagus in oil and two bottles of champagne. I can declare that in my life I had never had a meal that seemed so delicious." (*Ibid*, 172) Renneville also resumes another prisoner's account of the change in regimes. The man claims that under Governor de Bésemeaux:

Prisoners.. in the towers were brought, every morning, in a large basket covered with white linen, three loaves cooked overnight, weighing together a pound, fruit of the season, enough for the day, and two bottles of Champagne or Burgundy wine. At noon, they were brought a well-seasoned soup with a pound of boiled meat, the most succulent in Paris, beef, veal and mutton and a dish of stew. In the evening, they were given half a pound of roast meat, beef, veal mutton, or lamb; half a chicken, or a rabbit or a squab, or an equivalent stew, and always a small salad. Since it was impossible for a prisoner to eat so much meat, if he only had one meal, he was paid 15 sols for the other [*NOTE earlier – page 102 – he says 15 per meal, but that might be mistake for the daily price*], or if he was happy with one bottle of wine, they gave him seven and a half sous – others have told me ten – for the other bottle. Thus one could easily save 22 sous a day, and still live well. While today [*under Bernaville*], we only have two or three ounces of carrion a day, because one would think it came from the road rather that from the butcher. As to the wine, it is only that in name." (*Ibid*, 130)

The overall impression left by these accounts is that some prisoners ate very well and that most at least had some kind of meat. Above all, here, as with everything else in the Bastille, treatments varied enormously depending on a prisoner's status.

The General Dumouriez provides one last thought on the food in the Bastille. He arrived at nine in the evening on a Friday, when Catholics were forbidden meat unless sick. The formalities lasted too long for him to be fed by the Bastille's kitchen, so he asked that the major have someone fetch a chicken from a nearby caterer. —"A chicken," said the major, "do you know that today is Friday?" —"You are responsible for my keep and not my conscience. I am sick, because the Bastille is an illness; don't refuse me a chicken." (II, 258)

Appendix D. Pelliseri's letter to Major Losmes

The few sources that mention Pelliseri (with various spellings) do not so much as give his first name. Briefly, he was a Genevan financier who was probably imprisoned for criticizing Necker's financial policies. He seems to have been at least difficult, if not actually mentally unstable, and was transferred to the madhouse of Charenton before being released in the upheaval of 1789. For more information, see below.

The *Bastille Devoilée* refers to a letter which this prisoner wrote to Monsieur de Losmes (Antoine-Jerosme de Losmes de Salbray), a major at the Bastille (later massacred when it fell) and points out that it does not mention Necker. (*Mémoires de Linguet*, 56-7n). Coeuret provides the text of this letter, which is offered here as another view of life in the Bastille. Note that it is not addressed to the governor, De Launay, but to one of his subordinates, possibly because de Losmes was considered more compassionate than the notoriously unpleasant governor. Whatever his mental state or actual treatment, Pelliseri's tone is even more embittered than that of Linguet – which takes some doing:

> No doubt you know, Monsieur, that for seven years, I have been enclosed in the melancholy apartment that I occupy in this castle, ten feet wide in every direction of its octagon, nearly twenty high, placed under the terrace of the batteries, from which I have not gone out for a total of five hours on different occasions. It is horribly cold there in winter despite the poor fire built in that season, always with wood taken from the water; without doubt by a refinement of humanity to render useless the weak merit or the assistance of having a little fire to moderate the routine of the apartment. In good weather, I have breathed the air only through a window pierced in a wall five feet thick and barred with double iron bars, flush with the wall, outside as well as inside the apartment. Nor are you unaware that, from June 3, 1777 until January 14, 1784, I have only had a miserable bed. I was never able to use the cover, so torn is

it, devoured by worms, covered with filth and dust, and a sorry straw chair of the most common sort, with a back sinking into the seat, breaking shoulders, kidneys and chest.

To crown the discomfort of so sad a situation, every winter I have been brought only stinking foul water like that the river pours, in its floodings, into the ditches of this castle, where it swells its garbage and its uncleanliness with the filth thrown in the ditches by various households lodged in the arsenal as in the castle.

To top off all these atrocities, during more than three months before your arrival, I have been served nothing but the worst bread in the world, which has caused me great discomfort, accompanied, three quarters of the time, by all the left-overs and desserts from the masters' and the servants' table, and most often these stinking, disgusting scraps that sit and rot in the kitchen's closets.

Regarding bread, all through the spring, the summer, the autumn of last years, until the fifteenth of December, I've been brought nothing but the worst bread in the world, kneaded with all the swept-up flour from the baker's storeroom, in which I've constantly found a thousand lumps large as peas and broad beans, which showed clearly that this bread was specially ordered and that it was made up of bits or scraps which stuck to the wood of the machine where it was kneaded and carefully scraped after going sour. I, who am not hard to please, often I had trouble eating even half of the crust on it, quite hard and crumbling.

I've been itching several times to talk to you of this, but having won nothing in regard to the water, even since your arrival, and my complaints on this subject having led to the most disagreeable scene with Monsieur the Governor, I have kept silent so as to avoid any new altercation. I blame the violent jolts of pain and cramping I had in my limbs in the night of October 19th and which keep me in fear of a paralysis of the right arm and legs on this poor bread. I blame it as well for the sensations I've had several times and for the horrible deposits which formed in my legs, my feet and my hands all this winter, having constantly had six fingers of my two hands clenched up and my two legs from two fingers above the ankle and the five toes of my feet each pierced by fifteen to twenty holes. Monsieur the surgeon to whom I've shown them several times can confirm the truth of this.

(Coeuret, 23-28)

Berville and Barrière, paraphrasing the *Bastille Devoilée*, say that Pelisseri was transferred as a madman to Charenton in 1787 and only freed after the Bastille fell; also, that he had offended the Lieutenant of Police but that his interrogators led him to believe Necker was responsible for his captivity. (*Mémoires de Linguet*, 56-57). They and others dispute that the very respected Necker would have been responsible for Pelliseri's detention. Coeuret says: "Pellissery's only crime was to have criticized the minister Maurepas, regarding his financial operations, in a brochure entitled: *Errors and disadvantages of the loans of January 7 and February 9, 1777*....From the Bastille, having refused his liberty at the price of becoming a financial spy, Pellisery was locked up in Charenton and was still there in 1789." (Coeuret, 28). Maurepas however was Chancellor, not Finance Minister.

Bournon quotes official records that say he entered in June 3, 1777, and was transferred to Charenton on July 24, 1788. (Bournon, 294).

The anonymous author of the *Correspondance Secrète* says that important people petitioned Necker months after Pellissery's arrest to free him but that the prisoner himself refused, regarding himself as "a victim sacrificed to the public good" and preferring "captivity to a liberty subject to this condition" (which is never specified). (Letter XVI, September 30, 1777, 101).

Bachaumont says:

Monsieur Pelissery, a major financial speculator, ... had sent several different memoirs... to several successive comptrollers-general. He has just sent a new one to Monsieur Taboureau, to Monsieur Necker and to various other ministers. What it contains no one knows, but last Saturday they came to his house to confiscate every copy, and took him to the Bastille. Which makes everybody want to read this piece, which will only be that much rarer. We know that in general this author has very good views, but sometimes loses himself in crazy, chimeric theories. (*Mémoires*, June 13, 1777, 10).

Later, Bachaumont wrote: "It appears that Monsieur Pelissery's memoir attacks the financial operations of Monsieur Necker, and that that it is he who demanded his detention. No more is known." June 24, 1777. He mentions Linguet's claim that Pelissery had been in the Bastille for three years, and says that his only crime had been to criticize Necker's financial policies. (XXII April 9, 1783). But these public mentions did not seem to lead to his release.

Finally, in a note to the *Correspondance Secrète*, Lescure says that, like Linguet, Pellissery later wrote an account of his stay in the Bastille. (I, 66)

Bibliography

On-line versions of printed books are referenced as books, with the Web source listed after. Other Web references are grouped at the end. All sites were accessed June/July 2005.

THE BASTILLE

Book-length memoirs on the Bastille

Linguet, Simon-Nicolas-Henri, *Annales politiques, civiles et littéraires du dix-huitème siècle*. 19 vols. London, Brusssels, Paris, 1777-92.

> Linguet's account of the Bastille first officially appeared in this periodical, in the tenth volume, dated January 1783, 1-160. The numbering Linguet uses for each issue is not always clear from the text itself: mars 1777-sept. 1780 (I-IX, no 1-71).; 1783-1784 (IX-XII, no 72-96); oct. 1787-mars 1792 (XIII-XIX, no 97-179). In Volume VIII number 60 appears *after* number 61.

-----, *MEMOIRS of the BASTILLE, Containing a full account of the mysterious policy and despotic oppression of the French government, in the interior administration of that state-prison. Interspersed with a variety of curious anecdotes.* Trans., anon., Dublin: J. A. Husband, 1783.

> This is the original of the version presented here. It is one of several English-language editions.

----- and Jean Dusaulx, *Mémoires de Linguet, sur la Bastille et de Dusaulx, sur le 14 juillet / avec des notices, des notes et des éclaircissemens historiques*, ed. Berville and Barrière Paris: Baudouin fils, 1821

> A valuable French edition of this and another work that is richly annotated but, strangely, does not include all of Linguet's original text.

Masers de Latude, Henri, *Mémoires Authentiques de Latude: écrits par lui au donjon de Vincennes et à Charenton*, ed. F. Funck-Brentano, Paris: Fayard, [c. 1795].

> Though some incidents seem to be missing from this 'authentic' version, Funck-Brentano, the editor, was one of the major nineteenth century scholars of the Bastille and of lettres-de-cachet.

Renneville, Constantin de, *L'Inquisition Française*, London, 1713, 1715-1719, 4 volumes.

> The original version(s) of Renneville's work. I have not been able to consult it directly.

Savine, Albert, *La Vie à la Bastille: Souvenirs d'un Prisonnier*, Paris: Louis-Michaud, 1908.

> This is the version of Constantin Renneville's memoirs I have used here. Savine's numerous notes confirm or expand on many of Renneville's references. Though other authors also confirm many of his statements, Renneville has been accused of sensationalism and is not uniformly dependable.

Du Noyer, Anne-Marguerite, *Événement des plus rares, ou L'histoire du Sr abbé Cte de Buquoy: singulièrement son évasion du Fort-l'Évêque et de la Bastille, l'allemand à côté, revue et augmentée*, 2nd edtion, Bonnefoy, 1719

This is the standard account of Bucquoy's escape from two prisons, Fort-l'Evêque and the Bastille. Strangely, it is presented almost as an epistolary novel, in an exchange of letters between two women. No source I have found explains this, but despite first impressions it seems to be considered a serious source on the subject.

Accounts of the Bastille included in memoirs

Dumouriez, Charles-François, *La Vie et les Mémoires du Général Dumouriez*. Collection des Mémoires relatif à la Révolution Française. Ed. Berville et Barrière, Paris: Baudouin Frères, 1822, 257-296.

The general (who disconcertingly refers to himself in the third person) was arrested after going on a mission to Hamburg for Louis XV, who specifically asked him to hide it from the Duke d'Aiguillon, the Minister of Foreign Affairs. Aiguillon had him arrested. Dumouriez later said that he had played the part of Louis XIV's page, who had been punished whenever the boy king did anything wrong.

Gourville, Jean Hérault de, *Mémoires de Gourville*. Collection des Mémoires relatif à l'histoire de France. E. Petitot et Monmerqué, Paris: Foucault, 1826, Tome LII, 299-301.

Gourville's stay was very brief and is only mentioned here because of Linguet's reference to it.

La Porte, Pierre de, *Mémoires de P. La Porte*. Collection des Mémoires relatif à l'histore de France. E. Petitot et Monmerqué, Paris: Foucault, 1827. Tome LIX, 346-387.

La Porte, a valet of Louis XIII's queen (the Spanish Anne of Austria), was imprisoned more on her account than his, since Richelieu hoped to pressure him into revealing compromising information about her.

Marmontel, Jean-François , *Mémoires de Marmontel*, ed. Maurice Toureaux, Paris: Librairie des Bibliophiles, 1891, 3 Vol.; II, 126-140.

The rather light story of his brief stay starts with his conversation with Choiseul and goes to his release.

Morellet, Abbé, *Mémoires Inédits sur le Dix-Hultème Siècle et sur la Révolution*, 2nd edition, Paris: á la Librairie Française de l'Advocat, 1822, I, 93-99.

Another prisoner who took his brief stay (for a literary offense) in good part.

Staal, Marguerite Jeanne Delaunay, Baronne de, *Mémoires de Madame de Staal,* Collection des Mémoires relatif à l'histoire de France. E. Petitot et Monmerqué, Paris: Foucault, 1829, Tome LXXVII, 375-474.

Madame de Staal's account is as much about her political and romantic intrigues as it is about her experience of the Bastille, but nonetheless is informative on the latter. Like La Porte, she was caught up in her mistress' intrigues, and was arrested in an attempt to get information against the latter.

Retz, Jean Francois Paul de Gondi, Cardinal de, *The Memoirs of Cardinal de Retz, Complete*, Boston: L. C. Page and Company 1899, Book I.(on-line version at <http://www.ibiblio.org/pub/docs/books/gutenberg/3/8/4/3846/3846-h/3846-h.htm>)

The cardinal was not himself in the Bastille but visited people there several times.

Other sources on the Bastille

Arnould, A. and Alboize du Pujo, *Histoire de la Bastille depuis sa fondation 1374 jusqu'á sa destruction* 1789, Paris: Administration de la Librairie, 1844.

Anonyme, *Observations sur l'Histoire de la Bastille publiée par Linguet*, 1783.

Ravaisson-Mollien, François, *Archives de la Bastille documents inédits / recueillis et publ. par François Ravaisson Mollien*, Paris: A. Durand et Pedone-Lauriel, 1866-1904, 19 volumes.

This entire series is valuable, offering official reports from (mostly) inside the Bastille. The specific volumes used here are listed below:

-----, *Archives de la Bastille – Regne de Louis XIV (1663-1678)*. Paris: Durand et Pedone-Lauriel, 1870 Tome 4.

-----, *Archives de la Bastille – Regne de Louis XIV (1757-1767)*. Paris: G. Pedone, 1903, Tome 18.

-----, *Archives de la Bastille – Regne de Louis XIV (1765-1769)*. Paris: G. Pedone, 1904, Tome 19.

Bournon F, *La Bastille,* Paris: Imprimerie National 1893.

A remarkably thorough book that draws on previous works and, in the case of Linguet, often explicitly confirms or contradicts his assertions. Includes lists of all the governors, descriptions of all the positions in the Bastille, various lists of prisoners, internal regulations, etc.

Charpentier, François, *La Bastille dévoilée, ou Recueil de pièces authentiques pour servir à son histoire.* Paris: chez Desenne 1789-1790 9 livraisons en 3 vol.

A collection said to be largely based on documents found in the Bastille and other first hand sources. Barrière, in the French edition of Linguet's work, praises it highly and quotes it frequently. I have not had access to this extremely rare work, but have used a number of references from it provided by Berville and Barrière (and in one case Coueret).

Carra, Jean-Louis, *Mémoires historiques et authentiques sur la Bastille*, Paris: Fair+ J.P. Roux,1789.

Anonyme (J.L.Carra), *Mémoires historiques et authentiques sur la BASTILLE dans une suite de prés de trois cents emprisonnemens, détaillés & constatés par des pièces, notes, lettres, rapports, procés-verbaux, trouvés dans cette forteresse & rangés par époques depuis 1475 jusqu'à nos jours &c. avec une planche format in 4°, représentant la bastille au moment de la prise.* Londres, se trouve à Paris, Buisson, 1789. 3 vol.

These are two editions of the same work, which Berville and Barrière praise and reference in their edition of Linguet. I have consulted only their citations of it.

Coeuret, Auguste, *La Bastille 1370-1789 – Histoire – Déscription – Attaque et Prise*, Paris: J. Rothschild, 1890.

Genouillac, Gourdon de, *Histoire Nationale de la Bastille 1370-1789*, Paris: Roy, 1880.

> Coeuret and Genouillac's works are both general overviews of the Bastille and its history, apparently intended for a popular audience. Each however includes bits of information not readily found elsewhere.

Lusebrink, Hans-Jurgen and Rolf Reichardt, *The Bastille: A History of a Symbol of Despotism and Freedom*, trans. Norbert Schurer, Duke University Press, 1997.

> This modern work is primarily concerned with the symbolic importance of the Bastille and its fall, but includes some very useful statistical analyses in the first chapter.

LINGUET

Linguet: *Appel à la postérité ou recueil des mémoires et playdoyers de M. Linguet, pour lui-même, contre la communauté des avocats du Parlement de Paris*. 1780, gr. in-8vo, VIII

> I have not been able to consult this work, which Linguet refers to several times. It appears to be a collection of his legal pleas, offered in response to his dismissal from the bar.

_____, *Le fanatisme des philosophes*. 1764

> An early work of Linguet's cited in the introduction.

Biographies and studies

Baruch, Daniel, *Simon Nicolas Henri Linguet, ou, L'irrécupérable*, Paris: François Bourin, 1991.

> A French work I have only consulted briefly. However it appears to be a comprehensive biography.

Cruppi, Jean, *Un avocat journaliste du dix-huitième siècle: Linguet*, Paris: Librairie Hachette, 1895.

> A thorough and lively nineteenth century biography which however ends before Linguet's career as a journalist.

Levy, Darline Gay, *The Ideas and Careers of Simon-Nicolas-Henri Linguet*, Urbana Chicago London: University of Illinois Press, 1980.

> A widely respected work whose title fairly describes its contents: the author is as concerned with Linguet's (often paradoxical and complex) ideas as she is with his life.

Paskoff, Benjamin, *Linguet: Eighteenth-Century Intellectual Heretic of France*, Smithtown, NY: Exposition Press, 1983.

SOURCES ON 17TH AND 18TH CENTURY FRANCE

Bachaumont, Louis Petit de, et al. *Mémoires secrets pour servir à l'histoire de la République des Lettres en France, depuis MDCCLXII, ou Journal d'un observateur, contenant les analyses des pièces de théâtre qui ont paru durant cet intervalle, les relations des assemblée littéraires...* A Londres : chez John Adamson, 1783-1789, 36 tomes en 18 vol.

Correspondance secrète inédite sur Louis XVI, Marie-Antoinette, la cour et la ville de 1777 à 1792, ed. M. de Lescure, Paris: H. Plon, 1866.

Darnton, Robert, *The Forbidden Best-Sellers of Pre-Revolutionary France*, New York, London, W. W. Norton, 1996.

La Harpe, Jean François de, *Correspondance littéraire, adressée à Son Altesse Impériale Mgr le grand-duc, aujourd'hui Empereur de Russie, et à M. le Cte André Schowalow,... depuis 1774 jusqu'à 1789*, 2nd ed., Paris: Migneret, 1804-1807.

Somerset, Anne, *The Affair Of The Poisons: Murder, Infanticide, And Satanism At The Court Of Louis XIV*, St. Martin's.

LEGAL AND SOCIAL TEXTS

Jousse, *Traité de la Justice Criminelle*, Paris: Debure, père, 1771, 4 Volumes.

Chassaigne, Marc. (1904). L'Organization de la famille et les Lettres de cachet. *Revue des Etudes Historiques*, soixante-dixième année, 562-576. (Continued in 1905 issue, 60-73).

Frégier, *Histoire de l'Administration de la Police de Paris depuis Philippe-Auguste jusqu'aux Etats-Generaux de 1789*, Paris: Guillaumin et co., 1850, 2 volumes.

Funck-Brentano, Frantz. (1899). Quelques observations nouvelles sur les lettres de cachet en blanc. *Revue des Etudes Historiques*, soixante-cinquième année, 35-40.

Gallo, Max, *Que passe la justice du Roi: Vie, procès et supplice du chevalier de La Barre*, Paris: R. Laffont, 1987.

Langbein, John H. *Torture and the Law of Proof: Europe and England in the Ancien Régime*. Chicago: U of Chicago, 1976.

Mirabeau, Honoré-Gabriel Riqueti, Count of, *Des lettres de cachet et des prisons d'état*, Oeuvres de Mirabeau. Paris : Lecointe et Pougin : Didier, 1835.

Mézard, *Essay sur les réformes à faire dans l'administration de la justice en France*, 1788.

Préaudeau, Marc de (1927). Frantz Funck-Brentano. Les Lettres de Cachet. (review of the book *Les Lettres de Cachet*). *Revue des Etudes Historiques*, quatre-vingt-treizième année 174-175.

OTHER COUNTRIES

Delon, C., *Relation de l'Inquisition de Goa*. Paris: D. Horthemels, 1688.

Dellon, [C.]. *An Account of the Inquisition at Goa, in India; Translated from the French of M. Dellon, Who Was Confined Two Years In Its Cells. With an Appendix; Containing an Account of the Escape of Archibald Bower, From the Inquisition of Italy*. Boston: Samuel T. Armstrong, 1815.

Grube, Ernest J., *Muslim Miniature Paintings From the XIII to XIX Century*. Venice: Neri Pozza Editore, 1962.1968. Cited on "La Miniature En Orient", *The Oriental Rug and Carpet Site*,
<http://www.spongobongo.com/EKOM64.htm>

The Book Of The Thousand Nights And A Night. Trans. and ed., Richard F. Burton, (1885).

Magnan, Dominique, *La ville de Rome, ou Description abrégée de cette superbe ville divisée en quatre volumes et ornée de 425 planches en taille douce.* 1778.

Montesquieu, Charles Louis. *Considerations on the Causes of the Greatness of the Romans and their Decline.* Trans. David Lowenthal. New York: The Free Press, 1965.

Rycaut, Paul and Pierre Briot, *Histoire de l'état présent de l'Empire ottoman,* Paris: S. Mabre-Cramoisy, 1670.

C. Suetonius Tranquillus, *THE LIVES OF THE TWELVE CAESARS, To which are added, HIS LIVES OF THE GRAMMARIANS, RHETORICIANS, AND POETS.* The Translation of Alexander Thomson, M.D., revised and corrected by T.Forester, Esq., A.M. [on-line version at <http://www.gutenberg.org/dirs/6/3/8/6389/6389.txt>]

REFERENCE

A Dictionary of Early Christian Biography and Literature to the End of the Sixth Century A.D., with an Account of the Principal Sects and Heresies, Wace, Henry, ed.: (based on the 1911 John Murray edition), also ed. by William C. Piercy . [On-line version at <http://www.ccel.org/ccel/wace/biodict.html>]

Benét's Reader's Encyclopedia, ed. Brian Murphy, Harper Collins, 1948-1996.

Biographie universelle ancienne et moderne: histoire par ordre alphabétique de la vie publique et privée de tous les hommes.... publ. sous la dir. de M. Michaud ; ouvrage réd. par une société de gens de lettres et de savants

Chambers Biographical Dictionary, Centenary Edition. Ed. Melanie Parry, Chambers, 1997, 6th edition.

Chéruel, A., *Dictionnaire Historique des Moeurs et Coutumes de la France,* Paris:Librairie Hachette, Paris, 1899, 2 volumes.

Cotgrave, Randle, *A Dictionarie of the French and English Tongues,* Islip, London, 1611.

Diderot, Denis, ed. *Encyclopédie ou Dictionnaire raisonné des sciences, des arts et des métiers, par une société de gens de letters,* 35 vols. Paris, 1751-1780.

Encyclopædia Britannica. 2004. Encyclopædia Britannica Premium Service.

Seyffert, Dr. Oskar, *A Dictionary of Classical Antiquities Mythology, Religion, Literature and Art,* London: Willam Glaisher 1894.

Smith, Sir William, *Dictionary of Greek and Roman antiquities. Ed. by William Smith.* Boston: C. Little, and J. Brown [London, printed] 1870.

Thomas, Joseph, *Universal pronouncing dictionary of biography and mythology,* Philadelphia: J. B. Lippincott & co.,1870.

The Oxford Companion to Classical Literature, ed. M. C. Wats, Oxford University Press (Oxford, New York), 1989.

The Globe encyclopaedia of universal information, ed. John M. Ross, Boston: Estes & Lauriat,1876-79.

WEB SITES

"CHAPTER V - THE MONGOL CONQUEST OF CHINA", CHINA By Demetrius Charles Boulger (1893)
<http://www.nalanda.nitc.ac.in/resources/english/etext-project/history/china1/chapter6.html>

"Christian 2. · King of Denmark · Norway 1513-23 and Sweden 1520-23", Danish Kings ... and their history
<http://www.danskekonger.dk/eng/biografi/ChrII.html>

"Istanbul – Off the Beaten Track", Lonely Planet
<http://www.lonelyplanet.com/destinations/middle_east/istanbul/obt.htm>

"Prisonnier /Des prisonniers torturés ou executes", Electre,
<http://www2.unil.ch/iasa/iasa_c_est_aussi/electre/prisonnier/livre_elec/pris1_2.htm>

"St. John Chrysotom", Catholic On-Line:Catholic On-Line Saints
<http://www.catholic.org/saints/saint.php?saint_id=64>Armory of Old Regime (pre-1789) French Peerage
<http://www.heraldica.org/topics/france/peerage2.htm>

Castel Stan'Angelo <http://www.abcroma.com/Inglese/castel_i.htm>

Chéron, "BEAUMELLE (ANGLIVIEL DE LA), 1727-1773", CÉDÉROM DES OEUVRES COMPLÈTES DE VOLTAIRE Ó2005
<http://perso.wanadoo.fr/dboudin/zGalerie/La_Beaumelle.html>

La France Pittoresque: Quelques événements du 27 FÉVRIER
<http://www.france-pittoresque.com/almanach/2702b.htm>

Le Grand Dictionnaire Terminologique <http://www.granddictionnaire.com>

Marshals of France <http://en.wikipedia.org/wiki/Marshal_of_France>

The 1911 Edition Encyclopedia <http://54.1911encyclopedia.org>

The Columbia Encyclopedia, 6th ed. New York: Columbia University Press, 2002. <www.encyclopedia.com>

The Linda Hall Library History Of Science Collection
<http://www.lindahall.org/events_exhib/exhibit/ex_voyages.shtml>

Vergennes < http://rulers.org/frgovt1.html>

Worldroots.com: The Descendants of Countess Elisabeth von Nassau
<http://worldroots.com/brigitte/royal/kent/elisabethnassaudesc.htm>

Printed in Great Britain
by Amazon